October 2001

Dear Linc,

Mangia bene! Viva il
cuoco.

Tanti auguri per i
compleanni,

La Familia Visini

Stephanie Alexander
& Maggie Beer
TUSCAN
COOKBOOK

LAUREL
GLEN

TUSCAN COOKBOOK

Stephanie Alexander
& Maggie Beer

Photography by
SIMON GRIFFITHS

LAUREL
GLEN

Our warmest thanks to Tony,
who created everchanging and always beautiful
environments in which to live and work.
And to Elena and Peter, who with Tony made the
cooking schools a memorable venture.

ACKNOWLEDGMENTS

We would like to thank the following people who helped make our cooking school happen: Elena Bonnici, Peter Lortz, and Tony Phillips, who were the most wonderful, willing helpers one could ever ask for; Ichiko Noonan, who traveled all over Umbria and Tuscany to check out likely properties; Ann Parronchi, who did the organization on the ground, got us into the amazing Metro supply store, and lent us wonderful pots and pans; Diana Ninchen, who with Ann guided us through local markets; Paolo de Marchi, who traveled those roads three times to inspire us with his knowledge of Chianti, its wine and its character; Chris Butler, who guided us through olive-oil tastings; Peter James, of Negociants in Adelaide, who organized our lovely wines from so far away; Alex Belson, of Antinori Wines, whose winery, wines, and hospitality we enjoyed immensely; Anna Rosa Vasconetto Migone, who rented us the villa (which was located via the catalog of a Melbourne firm, Cottages & Castles) and was intrigued by the way we reorganized it but loved the result, and the Migone family, who occupied the other half; the Bischi family, who allowed us to visit their beautiful farm twice; Sue Graham, of Leggett World Travel, who organized all the bookings for the students; and Colin Beer, the best backroom boy ever.

We would also like to thank Simon Griffiths, for his inspirational photography; Caroline Pizzey, who as usual worked like the inspired food-loving editor she is; Beth McKinlay, for her beautiful "Tuscan" design; and especially our publisher and friend Julie Gibbs, for her enthusiasm for and friendship on yet another amazing venture.

BIBLIOGRAPHY

Anderson, Burton. 1994, *Treasures of the Italian Table* (New York: William Morrow)

Beevor, Kinta. 2000, *A Tuscan Childhood* (New York: Vintage Books)

Carluccio, Antonio. 1990, *A Passion for Mushrooms* (London: Pavilion)

———. 1992, *An Invitation to Italian Cooking* (London: Pavilion)

David, Elizabeth. 1998, *Italian Food* (New York: Penguin Putnam)

Field, Carol. 1991, *The Italian Baker* (New York: Harper Collins)

Eyewitness Travel Guides: Florence and Tuscany (New York: Dorling Kindersley)

Freson, Robert. 1992, *Savouring Italy* (London: Pavilion Books)

Gray, Patience. 1996, *Honey from a Weed* (New York: The Lyons Press)

Gray, Rose, and Rogers, Ruth. 1998, *The Café Cookbook: Italian Recipes from London's River Café* (New York: Broadway Books)

Hazan, Marcella. 1992, *Essentials of Classic Italian Cooking* (New York: Knopf)

———. 1983, *The Second Classic Italian Cookbook* (London: Macmillan)

Hellenaa, Robert. 1995, *The Sixteen Pleasures* (New York: Delta Trade Paperbacks)

Lasdun, James. 1997, *Walking and Eating in Tuscany and Umbria* (New York: Penguin Putnam)

Mayes, Frances. 1997, *Under the Tuscan Sun* (New York: Broadway Books)

Roden, Claudia. 1989, *The Food of Italy* (London: Chatto & Windus)

Simeti, Mary Taylor. 1989, *Pomp and Sustenance* (New York: Knopf)

Spender, Matthew. 1992, *Within Tuscany* (New York: Penguin)

Taruschio, Ann and Franco. 1995, *Bruschetta, Crostoni and Crostini* (New York: Abbeville)

———. 1993, *Leaves from the Walnut Tree* (London: Pavilion)

VILLA
DI CORSANO

AND
SURROUNDING
REGIONS

Firenze
(Florence)

C H I A N T I

Greve (in Chianti)

To LIVORNO
and the
Golfo di Genova

Tavernelle

Panzano

San Gimignano

Siena

L E   C R E T E

VILLA DI CORSANO

M. Oliveto Maggiore

To ROMA

Buonconvento

Montalcino

S. ANTIMO

Contents

The Olive Grove

The Farm

The Vineyard

The Banquet

The Road to
Tuscany

ABOVE The road to the villa.

OPPOSITE Ready in our cooking school aprons for the first students.

I N 1995 WE VACATIONED IN UMBRIA with family and friends. One lazy afternoon, as we luxuriated in hammocks, enjoying the vista of infinite space (and probably after a memorable lunch of bread, tomatoes, and rosé), we dreamed up the idea of returning to Italy for a longer period, this time to run a cooking school. We were certain others would be as enchanted as we had been (and still are) with the idea of developing an understanding of how best to enjoy the culinary and cultural richness and the sheer beauty of this extraordinary country. And so the seed was planted.

After much to-ing and fro-ing by fax, and with a lot of invaluable help on the ground in Italy, we secured two months in a villa tucked away among the vineyards and fields to the south of Siena. Neither of us had seen Villa di Corsano before, and we arrived with some trepidation in early September 1997, a week prior to the first of the cooking school sessions. So far from home and so much riding on the success of this venture!

It was an exceptional experience. And we believe that each of the thirty-six students who attended the three cooking school sessions had a memorable adventure—not just because we cooked wonderful food together every day, which we almost always ate outside in glorious sunshine, but also because the Villa di Corsano was so extraordinarily beautiful that we were surrounded by loveliness both inside and out.

An ocher-colored building sitting on a hill overlooking Siena, the villa was well protected by a drive of mature trees and surrounded by a structured garden of bay hedges, stone pines, and pencil pines. Red geraniums tumbled from terra-cotta pots in an inner courtyard, olive groves and grapevines covered the nearest slopes, and an herb garden established for us by our landlady, Anna Rosa Vasconetto Migone, ran alongside the swimming pool. The gardens and pool were protected by a bay hedge at least 10 feet high, the trimmings from which fed our grilling fire in the huge fireplace in the kitchen.

The villa had many treasures, both large and small, and each group discovered its own. Parts of the building date from the sixteenth century, with many changes over the centuries. Some rooms carried a simple crucifix, while the walls of others had exuberant nineteenth-century and early twentieth-century frescoes: cherubim tumbled among clouds, gentle hills and cypresses were seen through trellises, the Seven Virtues met with angels, fabulously striped fabric ballooned and draped, and noblemen greeted royalty.

ABOVE The original coach house entrance to the villa had been converted to a delightful bedroom that opened directly onto the garden. The windows were discreetly curtained with drawn-thread sheer cotton.

OPPOSITE This spacious and gracious dining room, with its worn terra-cotta tiles, huge fireplace, and dark beams, became the heart of our Tuscan experience.

NEXT PAGE Our first sighting of Villa di Corsano: clipped bay, stone pines, a soft ocher wall, and shutters all opened to the sunshine.

The floors in the main reception rooms were worn and uneven terra-cotta flagstones, polished to a dull gleam from more than a hundred years of use. It took a bit of getting used to as we slipped and dipped across them—but they were delicious in bare feet! Where there were no flagstones, parquet boards had the same lovely patina.

The furnishings were traditional, precious things everywhere—jugs, pots, plates, chairs. Shuttered windows opened out onto gardens and courtyards, and beyond to distant views of Siena and olive groves. Some windows had narrow curtains of fine white cotton embellished with intricate drawn-thread embroidery. The staircases were of stone.

On arrival at Villa di Corsano we found a cavernous cellar with buttressed arches. Anna Rosa told us that the villa was on the site of an Etruscan ruin and that the cellar remained from the original building, making it a thousand years old. It was cold and clean and empty other than for a lone bat. It was the perfect place to store our cases of wine.

Elena Bonnici, Peter Lortz, and Tony Phillips helped us set up the villa before the first students arrived, and then were on deck as helpers for the duration. They were the most wonderful, hardworking, and talented team one could ever wish to have on such a venture. Refrigerators that froze their contents, the daily laundering of a startling number of dish towels, the unusual ingredients that had to be tracked down, the trains, planes, and cars that required booking, and the interrogation of the butcher were all handled with great aplomb and much good humor. Their combined language, decorating, and cooking skills were invaluable.

The teaching took place in both the main kitchen and the sunny courtyard, our flow-over workspace, and by 12:30 most days the students were encouraged to have a glass of spumante or Moscato d'Asti while we made a few finishing flourishes. The cooking school sessions were punctuated by visits from Chris Butler, who led an olive-oil appreciation class, and Paolo de Marchi, the vintner from Isole e Olena, who guided us through tastings of his wine. Evenings were spent enjoying the *passeggiata* in Siena, or planning adventures further afield for the next free afternoon. We explored the wineries and medieval hill towns of Chianti, spent hours soaking up the art in San Gimignano's Collegiata and Museo Civico, discovered out-of-the-way restaurants serving fabulous food, returned twice to visit a truly self-sufficient farm (where everything from *prosciutto* to *ricotta* was produced on-site), heard vespers in the twelfth-century Sant'Antimo abbey, and returned again and again to the back streets of Siena, where little has changed, bar the odd brightly colored sports car, since the city was in its prime in the fourteenth century.

But perhaps the greatest learning experience of all was our weekly trip to the San Lorenzo fresh produce market in Florence. It was the quality of the produce that impressed. We had to redefine "in season" after our first market trip. The fruit and vegetables were *so* fresh that they had to be used immediately: when one is surrounded by produce picked when ready to eat this is exactly what one must do! This also meant that we could never predict what we would find in the market. If it wasn't ripe, it wasn't there. We couldn't complain about quality; the zucchini, tomatoes (in every shape and form),

→ *page 16*

OLD STONE AND WOOD

It seems impossible to

WORN SMOOTH WITH AGE...

LOOK ON ANYTHING UGLY.

ABOVE Cleaning cuttlefish.

BELOW There were three flights of stone stairs—beautiful but hard on the feet (Peter wore out two pairs of sneakers over the three cooking school sessions!).

OPPOSITE The "salon." It was a most elegant room. Tony's flower arrangements echoed the exuberance of the frescoes.

artichokes and so on were without peer. Our plan to shop weekly in Florence was soon deemed impractical. Instead, we made very regular excursions into nearby Siena or down the road to our local *alimentari* to resupply.

The uncertainty about what the market would offer us each week taught us all an invaluable lesson. Buying in season means being prepared to be flexible. Time and again we found ourselves replacing this ingredient with that, or changing the whole character of a planned dish, or creating an entirely new dish because an ingredient was unavailable or a new, interesting one had presented itself. This is the way the Tuscans around us shopped, and it is the way more of us should approach our own shopping at home.

The students made pasta and *risotto* and stock, and learned about unusual produce. We prepared cardoons and stuffed artichokes, and braised *cavolo nero* and flat onions, and made soups with bread, and bought white truffles and huge amounts of fish, and saved rinds from *Parmigiano-Reggiano*, and stuffed zucchini flowers. We gathered dry branches of bay (source of the bay leaf) for our 13-foot-wide hearth fire on which we grilled an assortment of food from *polenta* to squabs. Grilling over a fire—barbecuing—took on a whole new perspective: pale-green apple zucchini were halved and grilled, anointed with olive oil, as were chunks of squash, the huge *bistecche alla fiorentina* (T-bones weighing over 2 pounds each that were portioned after cooking), red bell pepper, octopus, and cuttlefish. "Mixed grill" fast became our favorite meal and seemed to sum up Tuscan food: fresh, unfussy, and delicious.

And while we shopped and cooked and ate, we talked. We talked about food and about "going with the flow" and using what one has rather than fretting if an ingredient is not available. And we talked above all about never compromising on quality.

And so the cooking school courses rolled on. After the third and final session, we were exhausted but exhilarated by the experience. We had not presented ourselves as experts in Italian traditions, but as two cooks and food lovers who respect any landscape in which we find ourselves, and who can help others gain the maximum joy and flavor from every meal. We feel satisfied in the knowledge that we have helped change the way in which our thirty-six students feel about everyday ingredients.

Now we hope that this cookbook will encourage you, the reader, to toss away preconceived notions of having to follow recipes verbatim, and to look for and use the best produce you can possibly find. And we also hope that you come to love the food, people, and beauty of Tuscany as much as we do.

USING THIS BOOK

The recipes collected here are those we prepared in our cooking school. They are grouped in each chapter in loose "menus." For every aspect of Tuscan food, there are no hard and fast rules about which should be served with what or when. And the number of servings per dish can be varied: the Stuffed Peppers on page 68 can feed six as a main meal or twelve if part of an *antipasto* platter, for example. So many Tuscan dishes can be used this way, making flexibility a key requirement for all cooks.

The bay hedge that gave the grounds of the villa elegant structure also fed our grilling fire, imparting a wonderful flavor to our food. "Mixed grill" became our favorite meal, epitomizing all that we love about Tuscan cooking: the best and freshest produce prepared without fuss.

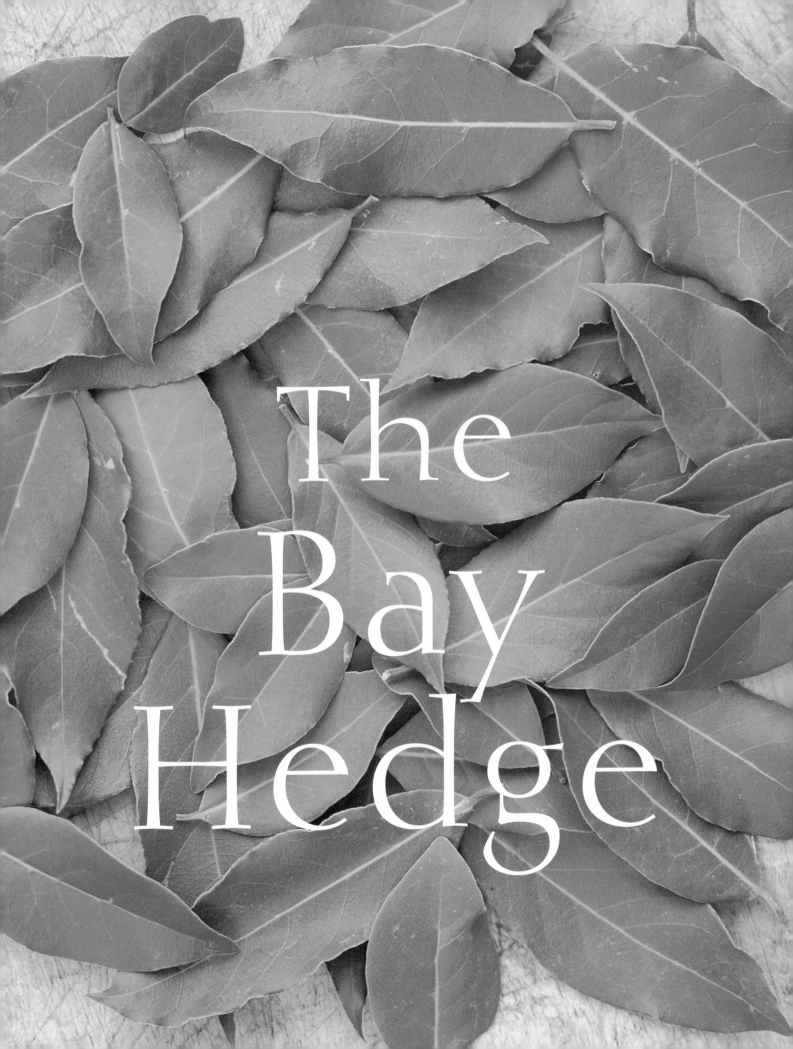

The
Bay
Hedge

PIADINI

These flatbreads are different from *focaccia* and the bread used for *bruschetta* as they don't include a leavening agent. In their book *Leaves from the Walnut Tree*, Ann and Franco Taruschio from The Walnut Tree restaurant in South Wales, United Kingdom, distinguish *piadina* dough from *crescente* dough, the latter containing milk and baking soda, whereas in *The Italian Baker* Carol Field describes a dough using milk and baking soda as *piadina*. Both authorities advise that a *piadina* is correctly cooked on a thick flat piece of terra cotta, known as a *testa*. A soaked shallow terra-cotta saucer intended for a fat flowerpot makes a perfect *testa*, as does an unglazed terra-cotta floor tile. While neither should be oiled before use, both need to be heated in a low oven or over a low flame before being used as a baking stone—this "seasons" the *testa*, ensuring it won't crack when the *piadini* are cooking.

Piadina dough is similar to the dough used to make *roti* in Indian cookery. Indian cooks often use half whole-wheat flour and half white flour, and they serve *roti* with curries. It is always fascinating to discover similarities of technique in widely differing cultures.

We made *piadini* frequently in the villa as they were ideal with *antipasti* (especially soft cheeses).

> 4 cups all-purpose flour
> 2 tablespoons butter
> salt
> tepid water

Make a well in the flour. Barely melt the butter, then add it to the flour with just enough lightly salted tepid water (about 1 cup) to make a dough. Knead well for 10 minutes, then wrap the dough in a cloth and put an upturned bowl over it. Leave for 30 minutes.

Break off about 20 pieces of dough the size of a small egg and roll each into a ¼-inch-thick circle that is 4–4½ inches wide. Heat a *testa* or heavy-based frying pan or broiler pan over coals or on top of the stove. Cook a circle of dough on the *testa* or pan for 3 minutes, then turn it over and cook for an additional few minutes. The *piadina* will have developed slightly burned bubbles, again just like a *roti*. Keep the cooked *piadini* warm in a cloth or loosely wrapped in aluminum foil while finishing the rest. They are best served hot.

MAKES 20

ABOVE AND OPPOSITE We tried baking the thin and very soft circles of dough in the oven on hot bricks in lieu of a *testa* but had far better results cooking them on a hot grill for a few minutes a side until crisp with burnt, bubbly bits. We kept the *piadini* warm in a folded dish towel in a basket until all were ready.

SALSA AGRESTO

STEPHANIE ❧ This almond sauce of Maggie's is wonderful with all manner of grilled things. I even added it to the remains of *Panzanella* (see page 181) and used the mixture to stuff artichokes and cardoons before baking them for a couple of hours in a moderate oven until meltingly tender. In another bid not to waste anything, one night the *salsa* was tossed into Maggie's squash *risotto* with leftover chicken and eggplant. The *risotto* was wonderful and looked great, speckled with rich orange and black.

Make *salsa agresto* within half an hour of serving as it oxidizes quickly.

1 cup almonds

1 cup walnuts

2 cloves garlic

2¾ cups Italian (flat-leaved) parsley

½ cup basil

1½ teaspoons sea salt

6 grinds black pepper

¾ cup extra-virgin olive oil

¾ cup verjuice (see page 219)

Preheat the oven to 425°F. Roast the almonds and walnuts separately on baking trays for about 5 minutes. Shake the trays occasionally to prevent the nuts from burning. If they are not freshly picked, rub the walnuts in a clean dish towel to remove the bitter skins. Let cool.

Blend the nuts, garlic, herbs, and seasonings with a little of the olive oil in a food processor to make a fine paste. Blend in the balance of the olive oil, then add the verjuice. The consistency should be perfect for spreading. If required, thin with more verjuice.

MAKES 2 CUPS

BELOW The formidable *bistecca alla fiorentina*, pictured here with grilled *radicchio* and garlic (see pages 107 and 111). These steaks weighed over two pounds each and are cooked whole before being portioned. The Tuscans season the cooked meat with salt, pepper, and olive oil. We tried it with anchovy butter—none of us had ever enjoyed a steak so much.

OPPOSITE The 13-foot-wide fireplace in the dining room became the center of our Tuscan experience. Tony was the "grill master" and perfected the technique of fueling the fire with trimmings from the bay hedges surrounding the villa. Simon, our photographer, took this photo from the area behind the fire, entered via a small door and used in times past by the family when extra warmth was needed in the winter.

GRILLED MUSHROOMS

One of the results of the extraordinarily dry autumn we experienced was a delay in the appearance of the wild mushrooms. The first *porcini* in the markets were actually from France. The second cooking school session had *porcini* from Sicily. Only in the third session did we have *porcini* from Tuscany. On a walk with Anna Rosa she showed us her favorite spots for collecting *porcini* and the less well-known but prized orange-capped *ovoli*.

This simple recipe turns cultivated flat mushrooms into something special.

flat, meaty mushrooms
olive oil
freshly ground black pepper
garlic cloves
sea salt
lemon juice
freshly chopped Italian (flat-leaved) parsley

Generously brush the mushrooms with olive oil. Grind pepper over them and add a few very thin slices of garlic to each mushroom. Place the mushrooms cap-side down over a moderate wood fire and cook for 5 minutes. Turn and cook the "gill" side for a minute or two. Remove to a hot plate, then sprinkle with sea salt, drizzle with the very best olive oil, and add a few drops of lemon juice and a scattering of parsley.

FIGS IN GRAPE LEAVES

Choose the freshest, most tender young grape leaves to wrap food for the grill. You may need to blanch them in boiling water or verjuice (see page 219) for a minute to make them sufficiently pliable. Verjuice enhances the flavor of the leaves, making this method particularly good when delicate fillings such as figs or goat cheese are to be used. Similarly, if the figs you plan to grill are a little green and firm, simmer them in verjuice for 5 minutes, then drain before wrapping each in an oiled grape leaf. Skewer the parcel with two toothpicks and grill over hot coals, turning once, until the leaf is crispy and the fig soft.

Grilled grape leaves also make a good bed for other grilled morsels. There is no need to do more than brush them very lightly with olive oil before placing them on a rack over the coals or on a hot charbroil pan. Turn the leaves after 1 minute and remove when crisp.

GRILLED QUAIL IN A GRAPE BATH

We grilled quail stuffed with grapes and sage leaves and wrapped in grape leaves very successfully in the first week at Villa di Corsano. Another time we chose not to use the leaves and instead rested the cooked birds in a "bath" of oil, verjuice, pepper, and grapes. We used the grape leaves this time to wrap flat circles of *tomino del boscaiolo* (a cow's milk cheese) and placed them on the dying coals of the fire for a few minutes only, as we'd been advised in the market, before adding them to the gorgeous *antipasto* platter. The smell of the wood fire was marvelous, helped by the plentiful supply of dried bay leaves used to stoke it.

If you are serving the grilled figs on page 24 as a lead-in to this dish, save the verjuice used to soak the figs to moisten the grilled quail for a flavor boost.

12 quail
Garlic Oil (see page 210)
salt
freshly ground black pepper
extra-virgin olive oil
verjuice (see page 219)
red grapes, halved and seeded
lemon wedges

Using kitchen shears, cut away the backbone from each quail and slip out the rib cage with your fingers. Rub each bird with garlic oil, then season and cook over a wood fire, turning often (about 8 minutes' cooking, depending on the heat of the fire). Make a vinaigrette of olive oil, verjuice, grapes, and pepper in a wide bowl or dish. Transfer the cooked quail to this bath and rest, turning once or twice. Serve warm with lemon wedges and *Risotto* with Crisped Sage (see page 28).

SERVES 6–12

ABOVE We loved it when our dishes changed because of the availability of ingredients. One day we boiled and shelled 2 pounds of chestnuts and tossed them with extra-virgin olive oil, seeded wine grapes, and diced *pancetta* that had been sautéed until crisp to form a variation on the "bath" for our resting quail. We served a fig wrapped in a grape leaf and grilled over the fire alongside each quail—a dish made in heaven. Like all good foodies, we also loved the chance to eat with our hands, enjoying the juices and the mess!

OPPOSITE Grilled Quail in a Grape Bath (this page) with *Salsa Agresto* (see page 23) and grilled apple zucchini.

RISOTTO WITH CRISPED SAGE

MAGGIE ❧ Anna Rosa planted a herb garden at Villa di Corsano for us the spring before we arrived. The sage was doing well despite the dry, dry year, but it always took great restraint not to pick more than the bush could take. Sage from our favorite vegetable shop in Siena was never bunched neatly as might be done here but was offered by the handful.

The Italians love this herb, and our time in Tuscany gave us a whole new appreciation of it. They simmer the leaves in butter, either just melted or browned, and they crisp them in olive oil; sometimes the leaves are dipped into a very light batter (sometimes with an anchovy fillet in between) and deep-fried. In each case, the result is a lovely aroma and an earthy, salty flavor—quite addictive.

1 heaping cup sage leaves

1 cup + 2 tablespoons butter

1 large onion, finely diced

2 heaping cups arborio rice

¾ cup dry white wine

6 cups hot Chicken Brodo (see page 213)

salt

freshly ground black pepper

½ cup freshly grated Parmigiano-Reggiano

Preheat the oven to 400°F. Arrange the sage leaves on a cookie sheet and dot each with a little of the butter, then bake for 5–10 minutes until crisp (any less than this and the sage will taste soapy). Set aside.

Melt half the remaining butter in a heavy-based frying pan or saucepan, then add the onion and sauté over a medium heat until translucent. Turn up the heat, then add the rice and stir well to coat with the butter. When the rice is glistening, pour in the wine. When the wine has evaporated, stir in a ladle of hot stock and continue stirring until the rice has absorbed the stock. Stir in the next ladle of stock and continue in this manner until the rice is *al dente* and creamy (a total of about 20 minutes). Remove the pan from the heat, then season and add the *Parmigiano-Reggiano* and crisped sage.

SERVES 6–12

BROWN BUTTER

Instead of crisping the sage in the oven, try dropping the leaves into a hot frying pan with a little cold butter. Swirl over moderate heat until the butter foams and turns nut-brown and the leaves are crisp.

Green Salad with Walnuts and Verjuice

STEPHANIE 🌿 Common names for foods can be confusing. What is sold in Italy as *scarola*, a large, opened-out round salad green with blanched yellow and pale-green leaves, each with a lot of crunchy rib, is sometimes seen at my Greek greengrocer's as "romana." And yet *romana* in Italy is definitely what we know as romaine lettuce. I amused a friend greatly at Florence's San Lorenzo market when I attempted to order two heads of romaine lettuce but apparently indicated that I desired two Roman men (*romani* rather than *romana*)!

> 6 handfuls salad greens
> freshly shelled walnuts
> 1 clove garlic
> VINAIGRETTE
> 2 tablespoons verjuice (see page 219)
> 2 teaspoons lemon juice
> sea salt
> ½ cup walnut oil
> freshly ground black pepper

Preheat the oven to 425°F. Wash and dry the salad greens and set them aside. Roast the walnuts for about 5 minutes, then rub their bitter skins off with a clean dish towel, if not freshly picked. Rub the cut clove of garlic over the inside of a salad bowl.

To make the vinaigrette, whisk the verjuice and lemon juice with a little sea salt. Slowly whisk in the walnut oil until blended, then add the pepper. Toss the salad greens and walnuts with the vinaigrette so that they are lightly but evenly coated. A handful of fresh green grapes would be an appropriate addition, too.

SERVES 6

CHILLED LEMON CREAM

BELOW The entrance to our village. New road rules and unfamiliar signs are part of the whole experience when traveling, and we soon learned to park Italian-style by simply moving barricades, bikes, and so on to give us room. We were highly amused when Aldo, our friend Ann's husband, told us that he takes no notice of red lights after ten in the evening!

OPPOSITE Tony found beautiful wild, tight, sweet blackberries in the market. One week there were red raspberries, the next golden.

We served this lemon cream in demitasse cups topped with the tiny, full-flavored wild blackberries and raspberries Peter found in Siena.

4 sponge ladyfinger cookies, broken into pieces
⅓ cup sweet wine or marsala
4 eggs, separated
½ cup sugar
grated zest of 3 lemons
1 pint heavy cream
Candied Lemon Peel (see page 69)
powdered sugar

Sprinkle the broken sponge ladyfingers with the wine. Whisk the egg yolks with the sugar until pale and thick, then mix in the lemon zest. In another bowl, beat the egg whites until stiff peaks form, then mix very carefully into the yolk mixture. Whip the cream and fold it into the egg mixture with the soaked ladysponge.

Spoon the mixture into ten 3½-ounce (100 ml) molds and freeze for no longer than 1 hour (the mixture is not meant to become solid). Decorate with chopped candied lemon peel and dust with powdered sugar. Serve with berries or Lemon Cookies (see page 32).

MAKES 10

EMON COOKIES

BELOW The annex: this courtyard was a favorite spot, not only for overflow classes, but for a drink, a chat, or to write in one's diary. Instructions on the day's workload often began here, with some students electing to do the outside jobs so that they could stay in the sunshine.

OPPOSITE We were delighted by these tissue-wrapped lemons—the lemons were so fragrant and juicy they hardly needed advertising but their beautiful wrapping made them irresistible.

Anna Rosa told us that one of the small stone "houses" used as a changing room near the swimming pool was once the citrus house. The lemon and orange trees were transferred inside in their pots at the sign of the first frost and would re-emerge in the spring. This solved something that had been puzzling us: the absence of lemon trees from gardens.

½ cup blanched almonds

¼ cup Candied Lemon Peel (see page 69), chopped

finely grated zest of ½ lemon

⅓ cup all-purpose flour

¼ cup unsalted butter

¼ cup sugar

1½ tablespoons milk

ICING

½ cup powdered sugar

orange or lemon juice

Finely chop the almonds and candied peel in a food processor. Add the remaining ingredients to make a smooth dough. Roll the mixture into logs 1 inch in diameter and wrap in plastic wrap. Chill for 1 hour.

Preheat the oven to 325°F. Slice the chilled dough very thinly and arrange the slices well apart on a cookie sheet lined with baking parchment. Bake for 10–15 minutes until lightly browned. Cool on a wire rack.

To make the icing, mix the powdered sugar with enough orange or lemon juice to achieve a spreading consistency. Ice the cookies when they are cool and allow them to dry.

CHOCOLATE CRESPELLE WITH MASCARPONE, FIGS, AND STREGA

MAGGIE ❧ This dessert or afternoon-tea treat is based on a recipe from a friend, chef James Fien. It became a great favorite of the team at Villa di Corsano—Peter also made it once by cooking the figs in the delicious Tuscan dessert wine *vin santo* instead of sprinkling them with *Strega*. Sublime!

OPPOSITE A strong aesthetic seems to be universal in Italy: everything was so beautifully presented. And there were so many traditional delicacies available. Our friend Diana brought us these delicious *biscotti* as a gift.

NEXT PAGE Tony sets the scene (and the table) under the elms for lunch. This was our daily custom, although on this occasion the antique chairs from the dining room had been borrowed.

1 tablespoon butter

⅓ cup milk

4 eggs

2½ teaspoons Strega (see page 219)

1¼ cups all-purpose flour

½ cup Dutch cocoa

2 tablespoons sugar

1 teaspoon salt

FILLING

½ cup dried figs

verjuice (see page 219)

2½ teaspoons Strega

7 ounces mascarpone

Melt the butter in a saucepan over a gentle heat and allow it to turn nut-brown without burning, then cool a little. Mix the melted butter, milk, eggs, and *Strega* in a bowl. Sift the dry ingredients, then whisk these into the butter mixture to make a batter. If necessary, add more milk to adjust the consistency of the batter to that of light cream. Rest the batter for 1 hour before cooking.

While the batter is resting, start the filling. Reconstitute the figs in verjuice—this will take about 20 minutes. Drain the figs extremely well, then chop them and sprinkle them with the *Strega*.

Pass the batter through a fine-meshed sieve into a pitcher. Heat a *crêpe* pan, then wipe it with a piece of buttered paper. Remove the pan from the heat and pour in a little batter, swirling it to spread it to the edges of the pan. Place the pan over the heat again. After a minute, lift the thin outer edge of the *crêpe* with a fine spatula and flip to cook the other side. Remove the *crêpe* to a plate. Repeat this process with the remaining batter. Allow the *crêpes* to cool, then trim them to an even size.

Mix the figs carefully into the *mascarpone*. Do not overmix as the *mascarpone* will separate. Pipe or spoon some of the filling onto the center of each *crêpe*. Fold in the ends, then roll up the *crêpes*. Chill slightly before serving dusted with powdered sugar.

MAKES 8

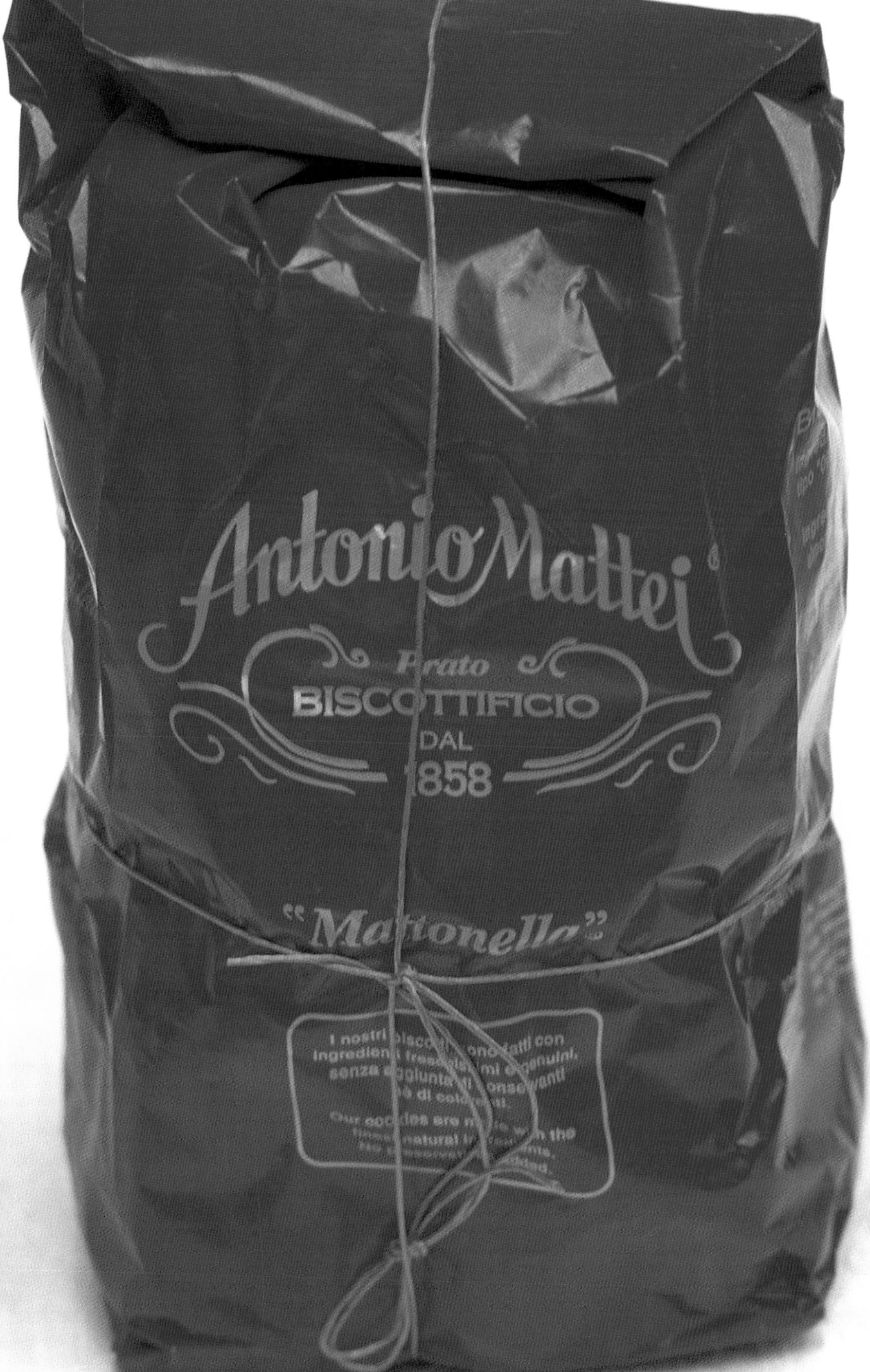

Antonio Mattei
Prato
BISCOTTIFICIO
DAL
1858
"Mattonella"

Zuppa pavese is the essence of simplicity but deserves some explanation. The following story is taken from Robert Freson's *Savouring Italy*.

. . . zuppa pavese . . . was invented for the French King Francis I after his defeat in 1525. On the way from Pavia to prison, his captors stopped at the farm of a poor man and asked for a meal, explaining that they had a king in their entourage. To honor such a guest, the wife brought out all the culinary riches she had. She sautéed bread in butter like a crostino, warmed some broth to boiling, slid in a raw egg that poached in its heat, dusted the soup with grated grana padana cheese, and set the meal before the king.

Points to watch: the serving dish must be very, very hot and the broth boiling. The broth can be spooned over and over the egg to ensure the egg develops a properly veiled appearance. Serve the fried bread on the side or beforehand with a savory topping.

A more sophisticated soup results if one adds wild greens or shredded lettuce sautéed first in a little butter. If the egg is broken up and stirred with the cheese and allowed to form shreds in the hot broth, the dish becomes *stracciatella alla romana*—but, we learned from Elena, the broth must not simmer after the egg and cheese have been stirred in or it will become cloudy and the egg will overcook. One can also poach wraps in some of the broth as a more elaborate first course, as is detailed below. The wrapping can be a quickly blanched cabbage leaf or, more delicately, a lettuce leaf.

This recipe is based on one of Marcella Hazan's from *The Second Classic Italian Cookbook* and is typical of an Italian stuffing.

ABOVE Anna Rosa Vasconetto Migone, from whom we rented the villa. She said that no other group had "lived" in the villa as we had, claiming it as a whole and using every nook and cranny.

> 1 chicken breast fillet, skinned, 9 ounces
> 4 tablespoons unsalted butter
> 1 red onion, finely chopped
> 1½ tablespoons finely chopped inner celery stalk
> 1½ tablespoons finely chopped carrot
> 2½ tablespoons fresh ricotta
> 1½ tablespoons freshly chopped Italian (flat-leaved) parsley
> salt
> freshly ground black pepper
> 1 egg yolk
> 2½ tablespoons freshly grated Parmigiano-Reggiano
> 12–18 lettuce leaves
> 4½ cups Chicken Brodo (see page 213)

Dice the chicken. Melt the butter in a frying pan and very quickly sauté a few pieces of the chicken at a time. Transfer the cooked meat to a bowl and allow it to cool before chopping it finely.

Sauté the vegetables in the same pan for 2–3 minutes, stirring, until softened. Add to the chopped chicken and stir in all the other ingredients except for the lettuce leaves and the *brodo*.

Blanch the lettuce leaves by dipping each one briefly into boiling water. Spread a blanched lettuce leaf on the work surface, then spoon on some filling and roll up the leaf securely, making sure the ends are tucked in over the filling. Pack the rolls tightly into a saucepan, seam-side down, and cover with just enough *brodo* to moisten them. Place a plate over the top to hold the wraps steady and simmer for 20 minutes.

To serve, heat the remaining *brodo* until boiling. Place 2–3 wraps in a heated soup plate and ladle over the *brodo*. Pass extra *Parmigiano-Reggiano* separately.

SERVES 6

BELOW This is a detail of a huge painting in the villa's grandest bedroom—it was wider than the enormous double bed over which it hung! The condition of being a resident of this room was that one had to close the shutters each afternoon to protect this work from the sun.

EGGPLANT LASAGNE

One night, after a long day in the kitchen, we enjoyed a late swim and an even later meal of salad and this absolutely delicious eggplant *lasagne* in the garden by the pool. The last light of the day turned from amethyst to a soft gray and then to inky black. There were no stars, but in the distance the lights of Siena twinkled.

Lasagne pasta sheets need to be cut to fit the size of the baking dish you plan to use. Remember when cutting them that the pasta will swell considerably with cooking. Cook a few sheets of *lasagne* at a time in plenty of salted water for 2–3 minutes. Float the cooked sheets in a large bowl of cold water; add a spoonful of oil to prevent them from sticking together. Before assembling, drain the pasta, well spaced, on a clean, dry dish towel.

½ recipe yield Maggies' Fresh Egg Pasta dough (see page 211)

olive oil

2 cups chopped grilled eggplant

freshly grated Parmigiano-Reggiano

BÉCHAMEL SAUCE

2½ cups milk

4 tablespoons unsalted butter

½ cup all-purpose flour

salt

white pepper

freshly grated nutmeg

CREAM SAUCE

5 unpeeled cloves garlic

cold water

2 cups cream

salt

white pepper

1 cup roughly chopped Italian (flat-leaved) parsley

Make the pasta dough as instructed, then cut it into 4 sheets to fit a 2½-inch deep rectangular baking dish (about 8 x 11 inches) once it has rested.

To make the béchamel sauce, heat the milk to the scalding point and set it aside. Melt the butter in another saucepan and stir in the flour. Cook, stirring, over a moderate heat until you have a smooth, golden paste. Gradually stir in the hot milk until the sauce thickens and is very smooth. Continue stirring until the sauce boils, then turn down to a simmer and cook for an additional 5 minutes over a gentle heat. Season to taste with the salt, white pepper, and nutmeg.

To make the cream sauce, put the garlic into a small saucepan and cover with cold water. Bring slowly to a boil, then pour off the water. Repeat this twice more to remove any bitterness from the garlic, then slip the cloves from their skins. Bring the garlic and the cream slowly to simmering point in the rinsed-out pan, then remove the pan from the heat. Check that the garlic is quite soft—if not, simmer it in the cream for 5 minutes. Cool, then blend the mixture in a food processor to make a smooth sauce. Stir in the parsley and taste for seasoning.

Preheat the oven to 350°F. Grease the baking dish and line it with a sheet of pasta. Cover the pasta with a quarter of the béchamel sauce, then cover this with a third of the eggplant and a third of the cream sauce. Repeat this layering with the remaining pasta, sauces, and eggplant, ending with a layer of béchamel. Scatter the *Parmigiano-Reggiano* over the *lasagne* and drizzle with oil. Bake until bubbling and golden, about 30 minutes. Allow the *lasagne* to rest for 20–30 minutes before cutting.

SERVES 6

FRESH TOMATO SAUCE AND LEFTOVERS

We added leftovers such as 1 cup *Pappa al Pomodoro* (see page 66), cooked squash, or even braised and chopped artichoke to this *lasagne*. Another good variation is to spoon a thin layer of fresh tomato sauce over the final layer of béchamel before topping with cheese.

STONE FRUIT IN SWEET WINE

This "recipe" is not new, but it is excellent. The end-of-season small white peaches were ripe but still crunchy and are often served this way. Any leftover macerated fruit was wonderful for breakfast the next day—reinforcing the idea that no good food need be wasted.

> stone fruit (peaches, nectarines, apricots, plums)
> sugar
> sweet white wine or sweet white wine mixed with a little Amaro

Choose perfectly ripe fruit. Remove the skins if using peaches, but leave the skins intact on nectarines, apricots, and plums. Slice the fruit into a shallow bowl, sugaring generously as you go and discarding the stones. Pour over a sufficient quantity of sweet white wine to thoroughly moisten but not drown the fruit—it should not be floating in liquid. Press plastic wrap down onto the surface of the fruit to cover tightly. Allow the fruit to macerate for at least 2 hours. Serve with Almond *Biscotti* (see below).

ALMOND BISCOTTI

These cookies are only cooked once, unlike traditional *biscotti* (*biscotti* means, in fact, "twice cooked"). If using apricots or plums in the macerated fruit above, chop 2–3 kernels from the cracked stones and add these to the *biscotti* mixture for a very special flavor.

> 1½ cups blanched almonds
> 2¾ cups all-purpose flour
> 2¼ teaspoons baking powder
> 1 teaspoon salt
> ½ cup + 1 tablespoon unsalted butter, diced
> 1 heaping cup sugar
> 3 eggs, lightly beaten
> ¼ cup coffee beans, crushed finely or coarsely ground
> pinch of ground cinnamon

Preheat the oven to 350°F. Roast the almonds on a cookie sheet for about 5 minutes or until a deep gold, then allow to cool. Finely chop the cooled nuts in a food processor.

Combine the flour, baking powder, and salt in a bowl, then cut in the butter. Mix in the remaining ingredients. Knead the dough for 2 minutes; shape into a rectangle about ½ inch high and cut into fingers. Bake on a cookie sheet lined with baking parchment for 25 minutes until browned and firm. Cool on a wire rack and store in an airtight container.

MAKES 20

ABOVE There was a tree on Fattoria di Corsano that supplied plums for breakfast and as an alternative to peaches and nectarines when we were macerating fruit.

OPPOSITE We also macerated peaches—what an indulgence!—in *vin santo*, Tuscany's luscious dessert wine. We had heard about the practice of dunking *biscotti* in *vin santo*, but didn't try it ourselves. Paolo de Marchi, the Isole e Olena vintner whose *vin santo* appears opposite with Almond Biscotti (see the recipe this page), echoed our own thoughts when he asked, "Why do such a thing to a fine wine?"

Such energy, such *bella figura!* We were certain the Italian women must have been born in high heels, so confidently did they strut over the cobblestones. The evening *passeggiata* was a true spectacle as it seemed the whole town paraded or sipped a drink in one of the inevitable outdoor cafés. Life is to be enjoyed in Italy!

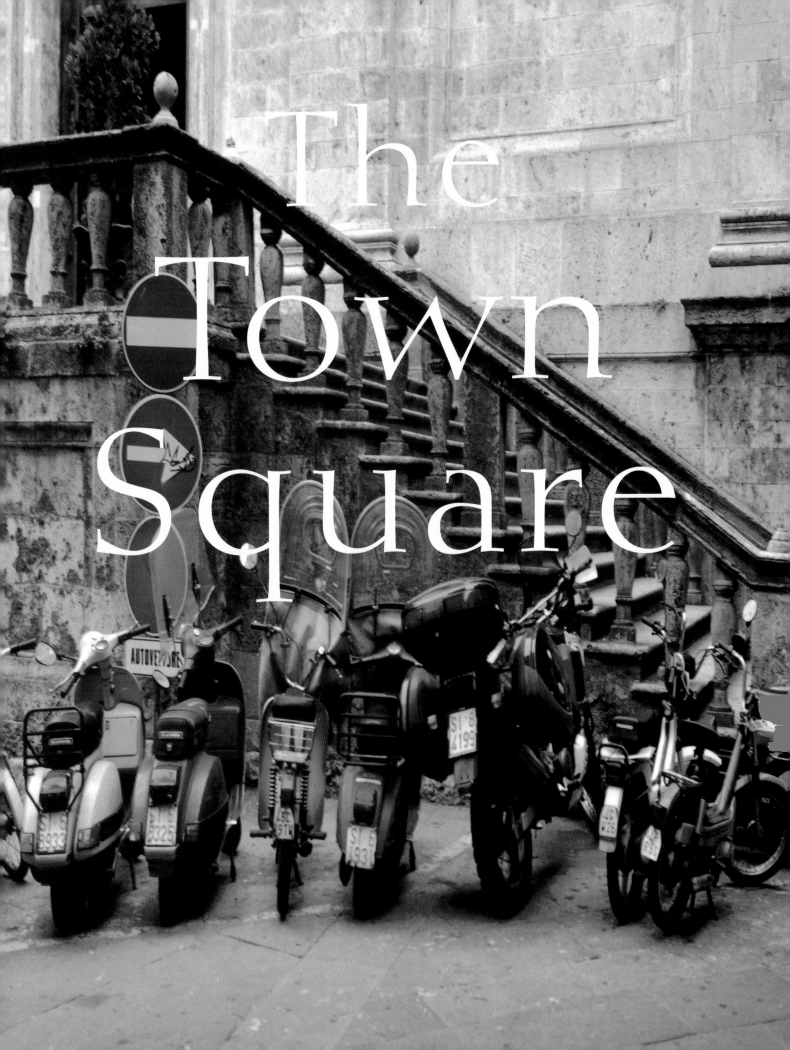

The Town Square

CHICKEN LIVER CROSTINI

BELOW Clockwise from left: Peter, Colin, Julie, Tony, and Lisa in Siena's overwhelmingly beautiful Il Campo. In early autumn it was a moving mass of Sienese and tourists either going about their business or else sitting on the brick-paving or at a *trattoria* soaking up the glorious sunshine. It was on such an occasion that an attempt at ordering *gelato* left the waiter greatly amused: our request was for fish (*pesce*) ice-cream rather than peach (*pesca*)!

OPPOSITE Supremely up-to-the-minute and yet with a timeless quality also, the Cantinetta Antinori, set in a fifteenth-century castle, was a favorite eating spot in the heart of Florence. We returned again and again to enjoy their unfussy but good food. We were intrigued to hear of their recipe for *crostini di fegato di pollo*: the chicken livers are lightly stewed with wine, *brodo*, anchovies, and capers before being puréed, then cooked a little more and packed into a pot to cool.

We enjoyed this archetypal Tuscan dish at Ristorante La Fattoria at Tavernelle, where mushrooms were added. We ate here in the garden and looked out over a vista of soft foliage, pink villas, vineyards, and hillsides guarded with cypress.

Liver *crostini* made regular appearances at the Villa di Corsano, but we were not accustomed to the local bread—the crust was so brittle and the crumb rather dry. We were puzzled how the Tuscans made their *crostini* with this bread. We tried and ended up with shattered slices. Later we realized that Tuscan *crostini* are rather more rustic in appearance than the French-style croutons we were making.

3 tablespoons butter

7 ounces chicken livers, cleaned and quartered

8 sage leaves, finely chopped

1 tablespoon red-wine vinegar

1 tablespoon tiny capers

2 tablespoons freshly chopped Italian (flat-leaved) parsley

8 slices baguette

olive oil

1 clove garlic

Preheat the oven to 400°F. Melt the butter in a frying pan and fry the liver with the sage for just a few minutes—the liver should still be pink inside. Add the vinegar, capers, and parsley, then increase the heat and reduce the liquid. It is important that this is done quickly so that the livers remain pink. Cool slightly and blend the mixture in a food processor using the pulse action or chop the ingredients finely.

Brush one side of the bread slices with olive oil, then crisp these on a cookie sheet in the oven until golden. Rub a cut clove of garlic over the warm *crostini*, then pile on the liver mixture and serve immediately.

MAKES 8

TOMATO BRUSCHETTA

Probably the most famous summer appetizer in Tuscany is tomato *bruschetta*, for which only the very ripest and juiciest tomatoes are used. The owner of Ristorante Nello La Taverna in Siena amused us by describing his experience as a visiting chef in a restaurant in New York. When he prepared the *bruschetta*, which, as every Tuscan knows, is bread, tomatoes, basil, and extra-virgin olive oil, the American chef proposed a few "improvements": a bed of arugula underneath, a shaving of *Parmigiano-Reggiano* on the top, a little balsamic vinegar, and some grilled zucchini to be layered with the tomato!

ripe tomatoes
extra-virgin olive oil
basil leaves, torn
sea salt
freshly ground black pepper
good red-wine vinegar (optional)
good, dense bread
1 clove garlic

Cut the tomatoes into a ½-inch dice, then generously moisten with olive oil. Add the basil leaves, salt, and pepper and leave for 30 minutes. Sprinkle on a few drops of red-wine vinegar if you like (we don't). Grill thick slices of bread over a fire or on a broiler pan, then rub the hot toast with the cut clove of garlic. Pile the tomato onto the toast and serve at once.

BELOW Drinking coffee in a street in Florence on one of our shopping splurges!

OPPOSITE One evening we had a short outing to Siena and chanced upon a part we had not yet seen. The Porta Romana is an impressive gate set into the ramparts that encircle old Siena, a reminder that this beautiful town was an independent republic during the thirteenth and fourteenth centuries, when it was at its most prosperous. The Medici crest was carved in deep relief on the gate. As we strolled along narrow streets outwardly unchanged since medieval times we looked up and into lit apartments displaying fabulous painted, coffered, and gilded ceilings. We imagined luxurious interiors.

PASTA WITH PINE NUTS, CURRANTS, AND ZUCCHINI FLOWERS

Inspired by a lunch at Ristorante Nello La Taverna in Siena, we "melted" zucchini flowers in olive oil to add to this pasta sauce (see photograph opposite). The flowers have a delicious and distinctive flavor and texture, especially where the petals join the calyx.

For a change, reconstitute sultanas in red-wine vinegar for an hour and use in place of the currants.

ABOVE Every day has challenges when one is a traveler. Where is it? How do we get there? What to do when we are lost and cannot find a sign?

OPPOSITE Pasta is eaten as a precursor to the main meal in Italy. In fact, in Tuscany pasta is eaten less regularly than in other parts of the country—bread or thick soups often appear instead—but it is still much loved. We particularly enjoyed it with "melted" zucchini flowers.

¼ cup currants
verjuice (see page 219)
¾ recipe yield Maggie's Fresh Egg Pasta (see page 211)
9 ounces zucchini flowers, quartered lengthwise
¾ cup extra-virgin olive oil
⅓ cup toasted pine nuts
6 anchovies, chopped
1 cup freshly chopped Italian (flat-leaved) parsley
salt
freshly ground black pepper

Soak the currants in a little verjuice for 20 minutes, then drain. While the currants are reconstituting, cook the zucchini flowers in some of the olive oil in a covered frying pan until softened.

Cook the pasta as instructed. Warm the currants, pine nuts, and anchovies in the remaining olive oil, then toss this through the hot pasta with the zucchini flowers and parsley and then season.

SERVES 4–8

OTHER IDEAS FOR PASTA

Toss ½ cup currants, ⅓ cup breadcrumbs sautéed in butter, ½ cup freshly chopped flat-leaved parsley, 2 finely chopped garlic cloves, and ¼ cup extra-virgin olive oil through hot pasta. Add anchovies and pine nuts and/or braised fennel, too, if you like.

Toss 1 cup toasted almond flakes, 2 finely chopped garlic cloves, ¼ cup extra-virgin olive oil, salt, and freshly ground black pepper through hot pasta, then add thickly sliced avocado at the last minute.

Sauté chopped garlic in a little olive oil, then add flat-leaved parsley, lemon juice, and cream to make a sauce and toss through hot pasta.

Herbed Pasta with Fresh Tomato and Red Onion Sauce

OPPOSITE The Sienese are born into one of seventeen neighborhoods, known collectively as the *contrade*, each of which has its own sign, set of customs, and even church and museum. Anna Rosa told us she was an Eagle—then there are the Snail, Panther, Forest, Tortoise, Owl, Unicorn, Seashell, Ram, Tower, Caterpillar, Dragon, Giraffe, Hedgehog, She-wolf, Wave, and Goose. The insignia of the *contrade* appear on the flags that are carried through the streets or hung from the walls during festivals. Ten *contrade* compete fiercely in the Palio, the frantic horse race run around the Campo each summer.

BELOW Fresh Tomato and Red Onion Sauce, seen here with plain pasta.

MAGGIE ❧ At Ristorante Nello La Taverna in Siena I had pasta with a tomato and garlic sauce of good simple flavors. The pasta was hand-rolled *pici*, a speciality of the region around Siena, and was so thick it looked like worms. My skills couldn't manage that, so I made my own version using homemade herbed pasta. The flavor of our pasta with the lusciousness of the ripe tomatoes equaled the restaurant experience.

> 2¼ pounds plum tomatoes
> 1 large red onion, chopped
> ½ cup extra-virgin olive oil
> 2 cloves garlic, finely chopped
> 1 sprig thyme
> salt
> freshly ground black pepper
> ¾ recipe yield Maggie's Fresh Egg Pasta made with herbs (see page 211)

Remove the cores and seeds from the tomatoes, then cut them into segments. Cook the onion in the olive oil over a moderate heat until softened, then add the garlic. When both are slightly golden, add the tomato, thyme, salt, and pepper and toss. Cook vigorously over a high heat until the tomato has collapsed and the juices have become syrupy.

Cook the pasta as instructed and gently reheat the sauce if necessary. Spoon the sauce on top of the hot pasta to present it, then toss at the table.

SERVES 4–8

SLOW-ROASTED LOIN OF PORK WITH FENNEL, ROSEMARY, AND GARLIC

ABOVE We also served the slow-roasted loin of pork with stewed artichokes (see page 72) and squash.

OPPOSITE We all enjoyed using the *mezzaluna*, the boat-shaped, two-handled knife that rocks across a heap of garlic or parsley with impressive efficiency. It is also much kinder on the wrists and forearms of the cook than our more customary thumping action.

STEPHANIE 🌱 The local butcher showed me how he would present a loin of pork for roasting. Rather than following my request to bone the meat, he released the meat from the ribs, but left it attached to the return bones. This way one has the advantage of the prepared meat settling back onto its bones where it is protected during the long cooking time.

¼ cup olive oil

2 cloves garlic, very finely chopped

2 sprigs rosemary, each about 3 inches, finely chopped

1½ tablespoons finely chopped fresh fennel leaves

freshly ground black pepper

9 pounds loin of pork, skinned and released from the bone

salt

¾ cup dry white wine

¾ cup water

12 chunks fennel

12 small onions

Preheat the oven to 350°F. In a small bowl, combine 2 tablespoons of the olive oil with the garlic, rosemary, fennel leaves, and a generous quantity of pepper. Open out the meat and rub the flesh all over with this mixture. Roll the meat back onto its bones. Rub any remaining mixture over the fat and sprinkle with salt.

Settle the meat into a stovetop-safe baking dish, then pour in the wine and water. Cook for 2 hours, basting every 30 minutes, adding the chunks of fennel and the onions after the first hour. Strain the juices from the baking dish into a pitcher and allow to stand for 10 minutes, then skim off and discard all fat.

Increase the temperature of the oven to to 400°F and cook the meat and vegetables for an additional hour. At this stage the meat should be perfectly tender and the vegetables cooked. Remove the meat and vegetables to a plate and keep warm. Strain the juices in the baking dish into another pitcher and allow to stand for 10 minutes, then skim off and discard all fat. Combine the two lots of juices.

Place the stovetop-safe baking dish over medium heat on the stove, then pour in the combined juices and allow them to bubble up. Scrape and stir vigorously to remove any cooked-on bits, then strain this simple *jus* into a warm serving pitcher. Carve the meat thickly, then moisten it with the *jus* and dish out the vegetables. Serve with stewed *cannellini* beans (see page 56). Any leftover meat is delicious cold.

SERVES 12

STEWED FRESH CANNELLINI BEANS

BELOW In one of the oldest parts of Siena, its narrow streets hung with the flags of the *contrade*, we came across small boys beating drums and twirling flags in true Palio style.

OPPOSITE Both dried and fresh beans are eaten with great gusto in a huge variety of dishes throughout Italy. But the fresh, creamy-colored *cannellini* and the beautiful carmine-and-cream *borlotti*, seen here, evoke Tuscany in particular.

MAGGIE ✿ The nickname other Italians give Tuscans is *mangiafagioli*—the bean-eaters. Perhaps my most wonderful bean experience was a simple dish of stewed *cannellini* enjoyed at the Cantinetta Antinori in Florence. A bowl of the most perfectly cooked fresh beans, ranging from white to cream to light green, was accompanied by nothing more than the bottle of oil already on the table. But this was nothing less than first-class extra-virgin olive oil, and the use of it was left to my discretion! I used perhaps a little more than most would, added just a touch of salt and pepper—and I was truly in heaven. I nobly offered my beans around, hating to part with any of them. At the same meal, Peter had a dish of bean soup with pasta, where the fresh beans had been puréed. Tony ordered tuna and beans for main course (he was delighted to find they were the same stewed beans I'd had), which came with a small dish of sliced baby white onion and olive oil. Yet again, simplicity won the day.

> 4 cups freshly shelled cannellini beans
> 1 fresh bay leaf
> ½ cup extra-virgin olive oil
> 3 cups Brodo (see page 213)
> freshly ground black pepper
> salt
> ½ cup freshly chopped parsley

Put all the ingredients except the salt and parsley into a wide saucepan or deep frying pan and cook, uncovered, over a gentle heat for about 30 minutes. Taste for salt when cooked, then add the parsley. Serve the beans on their own or as a side dish to meat (the slow-roasted loin of pork on page 54, for example).

SERVES 8

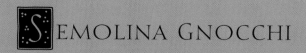

SEMOLINA GNOCCHI

MAGGIE ✿ For one of the cooking school sessions we weren't able to find fresh *cannellini* beans to accompany the slow-roasted pork (see page 54), so instead we made semolina *gnocchi*. The super-ripeness of the produce meant we could never be certain of what would be in the markets, so "going with the flow" and improvising soon became our motto—a good lesson to learn.

This recipe is from Elizabeth David's *Italian Food*. It was the first time I had tried making *gnocchi* this way—and I was very proud of the result!

> 2½ cups milk
> 1½ cups semolina
> salt
> freshly ground black pepper
> freshly grated nutmeg
> 2 eggs
> freshly grated Parmigiano-Reggiano
> melted butter

Bring the milk to a boil in a large saucepan. Add the semolina in a thin, steady stream, whisking constantly, then bring the mixture to a boil. Cook, stirring, for 5 minutes, then season with the salt, pepper, and nutmeg and remove from the heat.

Lightly beat the eggs with ¾ cup freshly grated *Parmigiano-Reggiano*, then add to the semolina. Pour the mixture into a ½-inch deep oiled nonstick pizza tray and allow to cool.

Preheat the oven to 400°F. Cut the cold semolina into wedges, then brush each with melted butter and sprinkle over a little more *Parmigiano*. Bake on a cookie sheet lined with baking parchment until golden brown, 5–10 minutes. Slide the *gnocchi* carefully onto hot plates as they are quite delicate.

SERVES 6

BRAISED FENNEL

This is a delicious side dish and can be prepared separately to serve with slow-roasted pork if there is not enough room in the baking dish for the fennel (see page 54).

2 bulbs fennel, quartered
2 tablespoons olive oil
2 cups Brodo (see page 213)
2 tablespoons roughly chopped fresh parsley
2 tablespoons roughly chopped fresh fennel leaves
freshly ground black pepper

Arrange the fennel in a shallow, heatproof dish or heavy-based frying pan that will take the pieces snugly. Drizzle the fennel with the olive oil and place the pan over heat for a minute or two to start the oil sizzling. Turn the fennel over. Add the *brodo*, then cover the pan with foil to delay any evaporation and adjust the heat to maintain a steady simmer. When the fennel is tender and there is still some liquid left, increase the heat to concentrate the juices. Remove the pan from the heat and shake it, then turn the fennel to coat it with the syrupy sauce. Scatter over the herbs, then top with freshly ground pepper and serve.

SERVES 4–6

BELOW A detour on a walk through Siena took two of us along steep narrow lanes of brick and cobblestone that meandered between stone houses carrying plaques listing their dates as 1619 and 1632. Children walked home from school for lunch. Elderly ladies strolled arm-in-arm. The smell of pasta water and mushrooms was in the air. And washing hung on the line.

PEACHES STUFFED WITH AMARETTI AND SPLASHED WITH BLOOD-ORANGE JUICE

Finding blood oranges in the market gave this wonderful dessert an extra lift, although ordinary oranges are what we'd use otherwise. (Julie's cocktails of blood-orange juice and Campari were just as big a hit!)

> 6 peaches
> 5 ounces amaretti cookies, crumbled
> 1 egg
> 2 tablespoons roughly chopped unblanched almonds
> 2 tablespoons brown sugar
> butter
> 1 cup fresh blood-orange juice

Preheat the oven to 350°F. Halve and stone the fruit, then scoop out a little extra flesh from the center and chop it. Mix the chopped flesh with the *amaretti* crumbs, egg, almonds, and brown sugar and pile into the cavities in the peach halves. Generously butter an ovenproof dish just large enough to hold the fruit neatly. Arrange the fruit in the dish and pour in the blood-orange juice. Bake for 30 minutes until the fruit is tender but still holding its shape. Serve hot, warm, or cold with the orange syrup spooned around.

SERVES 6

GINGER STUFFING
For another stuffing option, see the recipe on page 62.

BELOW Maybe some part of the sense of style that permeates Italian life is a result of living among historic grandeur and beauty and of appreciating the patina of age as much as the excitement of the new.

OPPOSITE Via de' Tornabuoni in Florence—site of fabulous shops (and fabulous people).

AMARETTI, ALMOND, AND GINGER STUFFING

This stuffing mixture for stone fruit differs from the one given on the previous page as it includes butter rather than an egg.

> ½ cup unblanched almonds (including 3 bitter almonds)
> 3 ounces amaretti cookies, crumbled
> 4 tablespoons unsalted butter
> 2½ teaspoons brandy
> 1 teaspoon finely chopped glacé ginger
> ¾ cup verjuice (see page 219)

Preheat the oven to 350°F. Toast the almonds on a cookie sheet for 5–10 minutes, shaking the tray regularly to prevent the nuts from burning. Set the nuts aside to cool, then grind them in a food processor. Combine the ground nuts, *amaretti* crumbs, butter, brandy, and glacé ginger, then stuff the peaches as advised on page 61. Place the peaches in a well-greased ovenproof dish, then pour in the verjuice and cook as instructed.

SERVES 6

BITTER ALMONDS

Bitter almonds, traditionally added to marzipan to give it its unique flavor, are not easy to find but most nut-growers have a tree or two, so keep an eye out when driving in the country. These nuts are only needed in minute quantities (large amounts are poisonous, in fact) and can be stored in the freezer, where they will stay fresh longer.

For a slightly different version again, add 3 bitter almonds to the ½ cup nuts and toast them as advised, then make the stuffing with the nuts, 3 ounces crumbled *amaretti*, ¼ cup dark-brown sugar, 1 large egg yolk, 3 teaspoons brandy, and 1½ tablespoons butter. Cook the stuffed peaches in verjuice as instructed above.

PAPPA AL POMODORO

OPPOSITE *Pappa al Pomodoro* is only as good as its ingredients: great tomatoes, good bread, and wonderful, green olive oil. Using leftover bread is typical of Tuscan resourcefulness.

MAGGIE ❧ There were times when I felt I couldn't eat another thing. On one such day, during a trip to Siena toward the end of our stay, Stephanie guided us to a restaurant a friend had recommended. At first I was a little disappointed as the waiters were formally dressed in white shirts and bow ties and were fluent in English. And there were lots of other tourists. Not in the mood for food, I ordered *pappa al pomodoro*—and all my uncertainty fled. It was as simple, rustic, and perfumed as I could have hoped. I added a dash of peppery, green extra-virgin olive oil as the Tuscans do, and I was entirely revived.

2 cloves garlic, finely chopped
extra-virgin olive oil
2¼ pounds ripe tomatoes, seeded and chopped
1 small handful fresh basil leaves, coarsely chopped or torn
freshly ground black pepper
salt
4 cups Brodo (see page 213)
1 pound day-old bread plus an extra slice for good measure, crusts removed
freshly grated Parmigiano-Reggiano

Briefly sauté the garlic in a little olive oil in a large saucepan, then add the tomato and basil and grind in some pepper. Cook for 5 minutes, then season with salt. Add the *brodo* and gently bring to a simmer. Cut the bread into ½-inch cubes, then add to the pan and cook for a few minutes, stirring. Cover and cook over the lowest heat for 30 minutes. Adjust the seasoning, then ladle into bowls and drizzle each with 2 tablespoons olive oil and serve hot, warm, or room temperature (but never chilled). Offer the *Parmigiano-Reggiano* separately.

SERVES 8–10

STUFFED PEPPERS

These peppers make a light meal when served with the potatoes on the opposite page, or a substantial first course. We also found that they are just as good sliced and served the next day as part of an *antipasto* platter.

> 6 red bell peppers
> extra-virgin olive oil
> 5 ounces day-old bread, crusts removed
> 1 cup milk
> 1 pound 2 ounces fresh Italian pork sausage
> 2 cloves garlic, finely chopped
> 2 eggs

ABOVE AND BELOW Choosing bell peppers and sweet pork sausages for our stuffed peppers.

Preheat the oven to 400°F. Halve the peppers lengthwise, then remove all veins and seeds. Brush the peppers inside and out with olive oil and bake for 10 minutes, skin-side up.

Reduce the bread to crumbs in a food processor. Reserve 2–3 tablespoons breadcrumbs. Place the remaining breadcrumbs in a bowl and moisten them with the milk, then leave for 5 minutes. Squeeze the breadcrumbs and discard the excess milk.

If the sausage is in link form, strip the skins from the sausages and discard. Put the meat and garlic into a bowl and work in the eggs and soaked bread. Stuff the peppers with the mixture, then pack them into an oiled gratin dish. Sprinkle each pepper with the reserved breadcrumbs and drizzle with olive oil. Bake for 20 minutes until the tops are golden and the filling is firm.

SERVES 6–12

STUFFINGS

Other stuffings could include leftover roasted meat, cold mashed potato, or grilled eggplant. The important thing is to season the filling well and to ensure it is not packed too tightly—the filling should be bubbling and juicy as it cooks, and not a solid mass.

POTATOES WITH CAPERS

The excellent yellow-fleshed potatoes we bought from the markets ensured this dish was a great favorite with everyone at Villa di Corsano. Look for waxy potatoes—fingerling, Onaway, yellow Finns, or Reddale would all be good choices.

> 2¼ pounds small waxy potatoes, washed well
>
> 2 tablespoons verjuice (see page 219)
>
> ⅓ cup extra-virgin olive oil
>
> ¼ cup roughly chopped Italian (flat-leaved) parsley
>
> 2 tablespoons small capers
>
> freshly ground black pepper
>
> salt (optional)

Boil the potatoes until they are tender, then drain. Toss the pan over heat for a moment to dry the potatoes thoroughly, then sprinkle in the verjuice and allow it to sizzle. Cut the warm potatoes in half so that they will absorb the oil and return them to the pan. Add the other ingredients and toss well. Turn into a hot dish and serve.

SERVES 6

CANDIED PEEL

This delicious and sophisticated after-dinner treat can also be chopped and added to cakes, icings, or puddings. Choose fruit with thick skin, and save the "shell" from breakfast grapefruit or when squeezing lemons (they can be frozen until you have a sufficient quantity). The beautiful, pink-skinned grapefruit we found in the San Lorenzo market in Florence were exceptional.

> grapefruit or lemon "shells," halved
>
> sugar

Cut each half shell into 4–6 pieces, leaving all white pith intact. Put the pieces into a heavy-based saucepan and cover generously with cold water. Bring to a boil, then pour off the water. Repeat this process twice to remove any bitterness from the peel, then drain well.

Measure the peel and return it to the pan with a scanty portion of the same measure of sugar. Cook gently until the sugar has dissolved completely, then cook steadily for about 1 hour until the peel is translucent. Drain the peel and dry it on a wire cake rack resting over a tray somewhere out of the way of ants. The draining can take a couple of days. Turn after 12 hours. When dry, roll the peel in sugar and store it in airtight jars.

ABOVE Siena is such an approachable city. One feels able to encompass it, to become familiar with its little alleyways and specialty businesses, to linger, to find a favorite corner, to return and be greeted as a regular by a smiling waiter.

We walked in many forests, some near the villa and some farther away in the wild Chianti hills. We imagined wild boar, but we saw pheasants and hare and deer. We also saw banks of tiny cyclamen  and crocus, and wild herbs and juniper bushes with ripe berries, as we hunted for *porcini* after the rain.

The
Forest

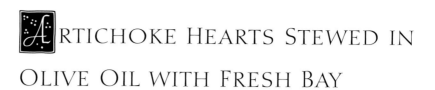

ARTICHOKE HEARTS STEWED IN OLIVE OIL WITH FRESH BAY

We enjoyed artichokes in a variety of ways: stewed on their own in olive oil, as given here, or with the addition of other vegetables as a salad, as part of an *antipasto* platter, hot with a simple dressing, or stuffed.

> *1–2 small globe artichokes per person*
> *lemon juice*
> *2–3 cracked peppercorns per person*
> *½ fresh bay leaf per person, torn in half*
> *olive oil*
> *water*
> *freshly chopped herbs*

ABOVE AND OPPOSITE The artichokes we saw in the markets positively bristled with flavor. On one occasion we mixed leftover *Salsa Agresto* (see page 23) with the remains of *Panzanella* (see page 181) and used this to stuff artichokes and cardoons that were then baked for a couple of hours in a moderate oven until tender.

Cut a third to a half from the top of each artichoke with a heavy-bladed knife and discard. Rub the cut edges immediately with lemon juice to prevent discoloration. Peel the outside leaves away until the pale, yellowy-green leaves are revealed. Peel the thick stalk, rubbing all cut surfaces with lemon juice immediately. Cut each artichoke into quarters and extract the hairy choke with a teaspoon or melon baller and discard, then coat all surfaces with lemon juice.

In a heavy-based enameled or stainless steel frying pan, stew the artichokes with the peppercorns, bay leaves, and equal quantities of olive oil and water until the artichokes are tender and the water has evaporated. Add a squeeze of lemon juice and stir in the fresh herbs. These artichokes are perfect to add to freshly cooked pasta or fresh or dried *cannellini* beans cooked separately.

BRAISED IN OIL

An alternative, if you have plenty of olive oil, is to cook the artichokes, bay leaves, and cracked peppercorns immersed in olive oil only at no more than a simmer, as if cooking a confit. Allow the artichokes to cool in the olive oil and serve with freshly chopped flat-leaved parsley, some of the cooking juices, and a squeeze of lemon juice.

VEGETABLES

If you want to extend this dish to become a complete vegetarian meal, add 1–2 small onions, 1–2 small potatoes, and 1–2 chunks of carrot per person. Stew these vegetables for 25 minutes in the olive oil as described above until nearly tender, then add the artichokes and continue with the dish as instructed.

PORCINI IN GRAPE LEAVES

In Italy during autumn every *trattoria* offers *porcini* in various ways. There will often be a simple still life at the restaurant entrance—perhaps a plate of mushrooms nestled on green leaves, with possibly a coil of *fettuccine* alongside. The same thing will be noticed in spring with asparagus and in summer with strawberries. There is no better example of how this country reveres its seasonal ingredients. This celebration of seasonal bounty was superbly defined for us by the display in the front window of a beautiful old café in Florence: here meringue *porcini* occupied a "woodland" setting alongside marzipan fruits of the season.

4–6 fresh grape leaves per person
2–3 porcini per person
2 tablespoons extra-virgin olive oil per person
1 clove garlic per person
1 boiled potato per person
1 tablespoon chopped sautéed pancetta per person
salt
freshly ground black pepper

OPPOSITE Sensible shoppers insist on inspecting each *porcino* very closely. Some mushrooms, and especially stems, can be wormy. Stems should be firm and dense with a smooth rather than chalky texture. Split in half or sliced across, the stems are delicious fried or grilled.

Preheat the oven to 350°F. Wash and dry the grape leaves. Wipe the *porcini* and cut out any damaged bits. Slice off the stems. Discard the stem ends with any dirt attached and slice the rest.

Choose a flattish, wide ceramic dish, preferably with a lid, that will hold the *porcini* in no more than two well-packed layers. Brush the dish with some of the olive oil, then line it with half the grape leaves, overlapping them so there are few gaps. Pack in the *porcini*, interspersing them with slivers of garlic and the sliced stems. Dice the potato and add it to the *porcini* with the sautéed *pancetta* and a little salt and grind over some pepper, then add most of the olive oil and cover with the remaining leaves. Drizzle with the last of the oil. Put the lid on and bake for at least 45 minutes and up to 1 hour. Remove the lid for the last 10 minutes of the cooking to allow the top leaves to crisp a little. Replace the lid before taking the dish to the table so that the guests get the full benefit of the aroma.

GRILLED PORCINI

Porcini are thicker and will take longer to grill, cap-side down to the coals, than field mushrooms (see page 24). If using the grill on a domestic stove, the longest grilling time will be with caps toward the heat source. *Porcini* can be sliced or portioned after grilling to be served on top of Grilled *Polenta* (see page 106).

FLORA'S CINGHIALE SAUCE FOR PASTA

BELOW Flora eschewed measurements,
preferring to use the knowledge of a
good cook, an intuitive understanding
of flavors, and her strong and reliable
hands. And how she loved an
audience!

STEPHANIE 🦋 On a perfect day in Chianti, we visited Ann and Aldo, who had bought a tumbledown property ten years ago that included a tiny church. Ann and Aldo knew that if they could find a church for sale the property would have a marvelous view, as the Church had been very astute at picking good spots! It certainly did this time. From every aspect, one's eyes drift over silver olive groves—the ground between the trees softly green after recent rain—and then on to cultivated fields and castles and churches and here and there another villa, and then beyond to thickly wooded steep hills, home to all sorts of flora and fauna.

Hard at work in the kitchen when we arrived was Flora, who has helped Ann for many years, a real character. She had consented to cook very traditional dishes for our group, and Maggie and I had been invited to watch the preparation. As we were exclaiming over the kitchen, she demanded of Ann, "Do you want to eat today or tomorrow?" We clustered around and watched her beautiful and very strong brown hands whisk fourteen

eggs into three pounds (13 cups!) of flour with nary a speck of flour cast onto the flag-stones. She slapped the ball of dough with great force several times on the marble slab, before twisting it round and round like a top and then rolling it out. Flora had her own rolling pin—it was at least three feet long, probably more. She divided the ball of dough in two and with powerful pushes rolled it and then flipped the dough onto the pin and rolled it again until it had stretched as fine as paper and covered the seven-foot-long dining-room table. It was left to dry, scattered with fine semolina. "If it dries so much the better, but we'll cut it when we are ready," said Flora, and turned her attention to the wild boar sauce for the pasta.

Few of us will ever cook *cinghiale* or wild boar, introduced from Hungary and the scourge of Tuscan vintners. Hare or kid goat would be a reasonable substitute, although the flavor of wild boar is much more delicate than either of these, surprisingly. Soak hare, if you like, but if you prefer a gamey flavor, don't. Kid does not need soaking.

Flora cooked with what she had on hand and judged the proportions herself. As Aldo does not like rosemary to dominate this sauce, Flora uses the stalk only—it is easily discarded.

Soak selected pieces of *cinghiale* in cold water, changing the water every hour for several hours until there is no more blood staining the water. Chop some onions, carrots, and celery, and gather some sage, rosemary, and a bay leaf. Dry the meat and marinate it in a glass bowl with the vegetables and herbs (known collectively as the *battuto*) and a glass of red wine and leave for 12 hours. Strain and discard the marinade.

Pour a good layer of olive oil into a heavy-based saucepan and add the meat and a little water, then "let it chirp away like a cricket" (as Flora said) over heat. Add more *battuto* (but not too much rosemary) and some chopped garlic. Cook for at least 1 hour until the onion has started to caramelize on the bottom, then add a glass of red wine. Stir in some homemade fresh tomato sauce and season with salt and freshly ground black pepper. Cook until very tender, stirring frequently. The sauce will be quite thick.

Remove the meat from the sauce and chop it finely with a *mezzaluna*. Return the meat to the sauce and reheat when needed. Serve with wide ribbons of *pappardelle*.

NEXT PAGE The law in Tuscany decrees that you can only rebuild to the dimensions and proportions of what went before, and that traditional materials must be used. Not only does this ensure *simpatico* houses, but presumably it also ensures the continued availability of skilled stonemasons and hewers of mighty beams. Today Ann and Aldo's house is one of the most beautiful we have ever seen. Here the table is set for an alfresco lunch for twenty people.

RILLED SQUAB

STEPHANIE ❧ The birds were huge—more than a pound each! Tony, who was grilling them over one of his special fires fueled with bay leaves, declared them to be not unlike pterodactyls.

I had a very prolific myrtle tree in the garden at Stephanie's Restaurant. It is one of the things I regret losing with the ending of that era of my life.

squabs
salt
freshly ground black pepper
olive oil
fresh bay, rosemary, or myrtle leaves

ABOVE This recipe began life as squab grilled over a wood fire and served with a blackberry and onion sauce (see page 81), but with no blackberries on hand, we had to think again. Instead, we made a sauce from crushed grapes for one meal, and on another occasion braised onions, olives, and the wonderful Tuscan dark cabbage, *cavolo nero*, as pictured here and described opposite.

To prepare each squab, cut off the first wing joint and drop it into a bowl. Cut off the head and neck, if still attached, and add to the bowl. Remember, do not cut the neck skin too close to the body as the skin will shrink on contact with the heat, exposing some of the breast meat, which will dry quickly. Gently push the neck skin back from the breast and remove the wishbone, which is embedded in the breast flesh. Work around each curve of the wishbone with a small, sharp knife, especially around the join of the two arcs. Feel the shape of the wishbone with your fingers, then ease it out and drop it into the bowl. Using kitchen scissors, cut up the back of the bird either side of the backbone right through to the neck opening. Drop the backbone into the bowl. Open out the bird, skin-side down, and remove the heart and liver (if still present) and add to the bowl. Rinse the bird under cold water, then pat it dry with paper towels and put it on a plate. Wash and dry your chopping board well and return the bird to the board, skin uppermost. Press firmly on the breastbone of the bird to flatten it further.

Season each bird with salt and pepper, olive oil, and bay leaves or rosemary or myrtle leaves. Allow the birds to rest, covered, at room temperature for up to 1 hour before grilling. If you have prepared them earlier than this it is better to refrigerate them.

Prepare the wood fire for cooking the squabs, then allow the flames to die down. Lift the birds from the dish, blotting any oil that might make the grill flare excessively, and place them flesh-side down to the coals and cook for 6–8 minutes. Turn and crisp the skin for another 2 minutes. Remove to a hot dish and rest for 5 minutes or so before carving and serving with Braised Flat Onions, Green Olives, and *Cavolo Nero* (see page 81) and *Crostini* of Squab Liver, Hearts, and Giblets (see page 86). Hot damp towels would be appreciated after this course!

BRAISED FLAT ONIONS, GREEN OLIVES, AND CAVOLO NERO

The flat onions we loved so much were quite exceptional—sweet and small enough to eat whole. They were sold in the supermarkets already peeled of their papery skins, although we found it much better to remove the first of the remaining layers as well. *Cavolo nero*, a dark cabbage new to most of us, is a bit hard to find outside of Italy, but well worth the effort! As well as having a distinctive flavor, this wonderful vegetable retains crunch after cooking, unlike other cabbages. Broccoli rabe or *rapini* may also be substituted.

> *flat or small onions*
> *olive oil*
> *Brodo (see page 213)*
> *green olives*
> *cavolo nero*

Gently braise the onions in a little olive oil and enough *brodo* to come halfway up their sides in a wide frying pan with a lid. Add the olives after 15 minutes, then stir in the *cavolo nero* cut into julienne. By the time the onions are tender, the *cavolo nero* will be blue-black and the *brodo* will have almost disappeared to leave a shiny, moist emulsion.

BLACKBERRY AND ONION SAUCE

We couldn't make this sauce in Italy because of a lack of blackberries, but have loved it as an accompaniment to squab back home.

> *12 pearl onions, peeled*
> *3 slices pancetta, chopped*
> *1 tablespoon olive oil*
> *water*
> *4 cups blackberries*
> *½ cup red wine*

Sauté the onions and *pancetta* in the olive oil in a frying pan. Add a little water and cook, covered, until the onions are just tender. In another saucepan, simmer the blackberries in the wine and then pass them through the finest disk of a food mill, discarding the solids. Add the blackberry purée to the onions and reheat just before serving.

SERVES 6

ABOVE *Cavolo nero* was very exciting. Stewed in oil with a little garlic, it became a *crostini* topping; shredded, it added mysterious dark notes to a good *minestrone*; and we also braised it with onions and green olives.

NEXT PAGE One night we heard vespers at the abbey at Sant'Antimo, near Montalcino, said to have been founded by Charlemagne in the eighth century but built mostly four centuries later. Its barrel-shaped nave and *campanile* glowed with light, so substantial and yet so simple. Inside, the abbey was extraordinarily beautiful. The massive columns were smooth and decorated in a restrained manner. And the acoustics were remarkable: the voices of the three Augustinian monks seemed to be pitched quite moderately and yet the round sound filled the space, each note lingering.

IT WAS AN OTHERWORLDLY

EXPERIENCE TO DRIVE

SLOWLY TOWARD THE

FLOODLIT ABBEY

THROUGH THE MIST.

BORLOTTI BEANS WITH PANCETTA

We served these delicious beans with the squab as an alternative to braised onions (see page 81), but they'd also be good with rabbit or even on their own with bread. The extra-virgin olive oil needs to be really flavorsome—remember that we had lots of fabulous Tuscan olive oil at our disposal!

We used squab stock since we had the bones, but one could also use chicken stock. If using squab stock, you may need to dilute it with a little cold water.

12 slices pancetta
2½ pounds freshly shelled borlotti (cranberry) beans
12 cloves garlic, peeled
squab stock or Chicken Brodo (see page 213)
water (optional)
1 sprig rosemary
extra-virgin olive oil
salt
freshly ground black pepper

BELOW Villa di Corsano's front gate.

OPPOSITE Detail from Taddeo de Bartolo's *San Gimignano in trono e i suoi miracoli* in the Museo Civico, San Gimignano.

Preheat the oven to 400°F and crisp the *pancetta* on a cookie sheet for a few minutes, then set it aside. Put the beans and garlic cloves into a heavy-based saucepan with just enough stock to cover (add a little water if the stock is particularly rich), then add the rosemary and olive oil and season. Cover the pan and simmer very slowly until the beans are tender but not mushy—this may take about 45 minutes. Allow the beans to cool a little in the liquid, then strain. Discard the rosemary, then toss the cooked beans with the creamy garlic cloves and crisped *pancetta* and drizzle with olive oil. Check the seasoning before serving.

SERVES 6

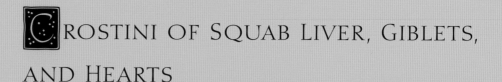

CROSTINI OF SQUAB LIVER, GIBLETS, AND HEARTS

We made beautiful *crostini* and *bruschetta* with the liver, giblets, and hearts of the squabs that we then grilled (see page 80).

3½ ounces smoked bacon, finely diced
8 squab hearts, halved
8 squab giblets, finely chopped
18 squab livers, trimmed
olive oil
1½ onions, finely chopped
3 cloves garlic, finely chopped
¼ cup red or white wine
¼ cup freshly chopped Italian (flat-leaved) parsley
salt
freshly ground black pepper
6 slices crusty baguette

Cook the bacon in a heavy-based frying pan until crisp. Remove with a slotted spoon and leave the fat in the pan. Sauté the hearts and giblets over a low heat for a minute or so, then turn up the heat and add the livers. Sauté quickly for 2–3 minutes, turning once, then remove to a plate. Add a few drops of olive oil to the pan, then add the onion and garlic. Cook for 1–2 minutes over a high heat, then lower the heat and cover the pan. Cook, stirring from time to time, until the onion is very soft and golden brown. Return the bacon to the pan, then increase the heat and add the wine and any juice from the meats and boil vigorously for a minute. Chop the meats quite finely and return to the pan, then stir in the parsley and season to taste.

Preheat the oven to 350°F. Brush the baguette slices with olive oil and grill on both sides. Pile the liver mixture onto the *crostini*, drizzle with a few drops of olive oil and reheat in the oven for 5 minutes. Serve immediately.

MAKES 6

RATIN OF SQUASH FROM THE GARDEN

We had planned to serve artichokes with the squab on page 80 but could find none when we wanted them. So instead we made a gratin of large chunks of squash, such as butternut, acorn, or pumpkin, tossed with garlic and *Parmigiano-Reggiano*. The gratin of squash looked sensational presented in one of Anna Rosa's caramel-colored glazed oval earthenware dishes.

> *extra-virgin olive oil*
> *freshly ground black pepper*
> *sea salt*
> *3 tablespoons freshly grated Parmigiano-Reggiano*
> *2¼ pounds peeled squash, cut into 1½-inch cubes*

Preheat the oven to 350°F. Put ¼ cup olive oil, some pepper, and a few flakes of sea salt into a large bowl, then stir in the *Parmigiano-Reggiano*. Toss the squash with this mixture until well coated. Choose a shallow gratin dish into which the squash will fit snugly and brush with olive oil. Pile in the squash and bake for 45 minutes to 1 hour. If the cheese browns before the squash is tender, cover the dish with aluminum foil for the last 15 minutes of cooking.

SERVES 6

TOMATO SAUCE
A little leftover homemade tomato sauce can be stirred through the squash thus prepared, as could Caramelized Onions (see page 194).

CHESTNUT HONEY SEMIFREDDO

On our first morning at Villa di Corsano, our friend Ann arrived with a large basket piled with goodies: the reddest tomatoes we'd ever seen, sage, lettuce, great bread, a huge bottle of extra-virgin olive oil from her own olives, a bottle of her own red-wine vinegar, and a jar of thick and luscious chestnut honey. The essence of Tuscany in a basket!

Ann told us that an old man named Alfredo turned up one day ten years ago at the restored farmhouse in which she and her family live and informed her that they needed a hive and that he had always made the honey for the farm's previous owners. He has continued to do so ever since.

If you can't find chestnut honey, any well-flavored honey will do.

½ cup chestnut honey
2½ cups whipping cream, chilled
2 small pinches lavender blossom

ABOVE A sprig of the highly perfumed lavender from the villa's garden went into our *semifreddo*.

OPPOSITE Barely frozen, this simple dessert was much admired. Lightly cooked figs, picked when perfectly ripe on the day they were to be served, accompanied the *semifreddo*.

Line six 4-ounce (125 ml) pudding molds with baking parchment. Gently warm the chestnut honey with ⅓ cup of the chilled cream and the lavender blossom. Whip the remaining cream very firmly and gently fold the melted honey mixture into it. Divide among the prepared molds and freeze for a few hours until firm.

Turn the *semifreddo* out of each mold and remove the baking parchment. Serve with Figs Stewed in *Amaro* Syrup (see page 90). The *semifreddo* should not be too hard when it is served, so remove it from the freezer and allow it to rest if dinner has taken longer than anticipated.

SERVES 6

FIGS, GRAPES, AND WALNUTS

Instead of serving the *semifreddo* with the *Amaro* figs, try melting 2 tablespoons lavender-infused honey in 2–3 tablespoons water over gentle heat. Add 2 cups halved and seeded grapes, peeled and halved figs, and walnut halves to the syrup to warm through.

FIGS STEWED IN AMARO SYRUP

BELOW The knocker on the front door of the villa.

OPPOSITE These nameless figs resemble the deep-red flushed variety we know as black Mission figs. The tree at the villa had just enough fruit to keep us going, the crop conveniently ripening bit by bit.

We picked figs an hour before lunch one day and gently stewed them in a syrup flavored with the digestif *Amaro*. These were magnificent served with softly set honey *semifreddo* (see page 88).

1 cup sugar
1½ cups verjuice (see page 219)
½ vanilla bean, split
12 large figs, peeled
½ cup Amaro
¼ cup thick cream or mascarpone (optional)

Put the sugar, verjuice, and vanilla bean into a large saucepan and heat gently until the sugar has dissolved. Add the figs and simmer gently, covered, for 5 minutes until tender, then let the figs cool in the syrup. Add the *Amaro* and leave for 30 minutes. Serve the figs and their juices alongside honey *semifreddo* (see page 88) or on a plate drizzled with cream or *mascarpone*.

SERVES 6

RISOTTO RADICCHIO

MAGGIE ❧ I love making *risotto*—I find the process tremendously comforting, a bit like making pasta. It was interesting how responsive everyone at Villa di Corsano was when *risotto* was offered. But the small kitchen meant that serving time was pressured if extra people wanted to be involved since *risotto* is best made from beginning to end without a break. I took the *risotto* to as close a stage as I could without spoiling it during the class, and then would let the most persistent person in to see it "come together!"

Most popular of all our *risotti* was this one made with *radicchio*. One day we made it with chicken stock; another day we used fish stock. Both were great. The deep red of the *radicchio* diffused to a rusty-pink in the cooking, and the marriage of the stock, *radicchio*, and butter produced a bittersweet flavor.

> *6 cups Chicken Brodo (see page 213)*
> *1 pound 2 ounces radicchio*
> *1 large onion, finely diced*
> *2½ tablespoons olive oil*
> *6 tablespoons butter*
> *2 heaping cups arborio rice*
> *⅔ cup white wine*
> *salt*
> *⅔ cup freshly grated Parmigiano-Reggiano*
> *extra 1–2 tablespoons butter (optional)*
> *freshly ground black pepper*

Put the *brodo* on the burner. Separate the leaves of the *radicchio* and wash them well, then drain and pat dry. Bunch together and cut into ¼-inch-wide strips.

In a deep frying pan or saucepan, sauté the onion in the olive oil and butter until golden. Add the chopped *radicchio* and toss to coat. Turn up the heat, then add the rice and toss to coat. Add the wine and allow it to evaporate. Season with salt.

Add a ladleful of the hot *brodo* to the rice and stir until incorporated. Continue this process, stirring continuously, until all the broth has been used and the rice is cooked but firm (it should not have a chalky center). This will take about 20 minutes. The last ladleful of *brodo* won't be completely absorbed, giving the *risotto* a slightly runny consistency.

Remove the pan from the heat, then stir in the *Parmigiano-Reggiano* and add the extra butter, if desired. Add pepper and check the salt, then serve.

SERVES 6

OPPOSITE One day we changed the character of our *Risotto Radicchio* by using Fish *Brodo* (see page 214), simply because we had run out of chicken stock. We served sardine fritters on top to give an additional fishy focus. This version went on to become a favorite in each of the cooking school sessions.

ELENA'S TIRAMI SU

Elena, one of the team, is a splendid and imaginative cook with special gifts for pastry and bread-making. Her sunny, happy personality that is also "a bit salty," as she describes it, is a joy, and she related well to all our guests, especially those who were more withdrawn or anxious. She made this *tirami su* as we had so much *mascarpone* (we loved the Italian *mascarpone*—it was so creamy and smooth and rich!) and as a treat for the team. It was such a delicious dessert that she was asked to make it again on at least two other occasions.

13 ounces sponge ladyfinger cookies (about 24)
2 cups cold strong black coffee
7 ounces grated bittersweet chocolate
1 pound 2 ounces mascarpone
Dutch cocoa
extra grated bittersweet chocolate
ZABAGLIONE
6 egg yolks
⅓ cup sugar
½ cup brandy

To make the *zabaglione*, whisk the egg yolks, sugar, and brandy in a bowl over a saucepan of simmering water until thick. Remove the bowl from the heat and continue to whisk until the mixture has cooled. In another bowl, whisk the *mascarpone* until softened a little, then fold it into the cooled *zabaglione*.

Arrange half the sponge ladyfingers over the base of an attractive bowl (2-quart capacity), then sprinkle half the coffee and half the chocolate over them. Spoon in half the *zabaglione-mascarpone* mixture and spread it over the sponge layer. Repeat this process to fill the bowl, then sift the cocoa over the final layer and top with grated chocolate. Refrigerate for 2 hours before serving.

SERVES 8

ABOVE Stocking the woodpile became one of the students' daily tasks. It was enjoyable collecting twigs in the nearby woods, and there were always wild mushrooms to look for. The bay hedges surrounding the villa were trimmed regularly—small logs of bay measuring 2–3 inches in diameter formed the basis of our grilling fires.

OPPOSITE Corner detail of the fresco depicting the Seven Virtues, on the walls of Stephanie's bedroom.

San Lorenzo is a true people's market. Like all Italian markets, it is found at the heart of the city, which says much about the importance this country places on its fresh produce. Easily accessed by pedestrians, impossible to reach  by car, everything is gathered under one beautiful roof. The produce is of splendid quality, and the market attracts many tourists as well as the food-loving citizens of Florence.

The Market

PANETTONE

Elena baked *panettone* one morning for us to enjoy for breakfast before heading off to the market, and also cooked a pan of damson plums to have with yogurt. There was a tree laden with plums on the edge of the property, and we helped ourselves, noticing the fruit was dropping.

ABOVE Our breakfast *panettone*.

OPPOSITE Detail from *Effetti del Buongoverno*, by Lorenzetti (1319–48), Palazzo Pubblico, Siena.

⅓ cup warm water

1⅔ tablespoons instant dried yeast or 3⅓ tablespoons fresh yeast

¼ cup sugar

6 egg yolks

1 drop pure vanilla

grated zest of 1 lemon

½ teaspoon salt

¾ cup unsalted butter

2½–2¾ cups all-purpose flour

½ cup chopped candied orange peel

½ cup sultanas

Mix the warm water, yeast, and 1 tablespoon of the sugar in a bowl and leave until it froths, about 15 minutes. In another bowl, whisk the egg yolks, vanilla, zest, salt, and remaining sugar until pale and thick, then add the yeast mixture. Gently heat ⅓ cup of the butter until barely melted. Gradually add the flour to the egg mixture, starting with 1½ cups, then add the butter. Finally, mix in the remaining flour (you may not need it all— the mixture should be neither sticky nor dry). Knead the dough for 10 minutes until soft and elastic. Put the dough into a lightly greased bowl, then cover it with a dish towel and leave in a draft-free spot to prove for 1 hour.

Punch down the dough, then press it into a rectangle. Scatter the peel and sultanas over the dough, then cover it with a dish towel and leave it to rise for another 30 minutes. Preheat the oven to 400°F and butter a round 6-inch cake pan that is 3 inches deep.

Carefully transfer the risen dough to the cake pan, then melt the remaining butter and brush the top with it. Bake for 10 minutes. Reduce the oven temperature to 350°F and brush the loaf with butter again. Cook for an additional 30–35 minutes, then turn off the oven and leave the *panettone* to cool in it. Serve as is, or toasted for a luxurious breakfast.

SCRAMBLED EGGS ON TOAST WITH TRUFFLES

BELOW These small *porcini* were marvelous for making *risotto* or for adding to sauces. They were not always cheap, so this was a serious purchase.

OPPOSITE Black and white *tartufi* in the San Lorenzo market in Florence. We arrived in Italy a little before the truffle season really started, and on our first visit to market our favorite stall was the only one to have any for sale (and then the white ones were from Piedmont rather than the still-dry Tuscany).

We readied ourselves for a trip into Siena with family and friends by having scrambled eggs with white truffles for brunch. "Truffles again," sighed Tony. "Three meals in a row!" The truffles had nestled among the eggs overnight and the shells as well as the eggs themselves were significantly scented.

> 10 farm-fresh eggs
> ½ cup cream
> 2–3 tablespoons butter
> salt
> freshly ground black pepper
> as much leftover truffle as you have!

Whisk the eggs in a bowl, then add the cream and half the butter cut into tiny dice, then season. Heat the remaining butter in a heavy-based frying pan. Pour in the egg mixture and turn the heat as low as possible. Give the mixture a stir as you see it start to coagulate, then stir only as much as you need to to bring it together slowly, making sure you bring the cooked egg to the top of the pan. Remove the pan from the heat before the egg has set completely. Have warm plates at the ready and toast buttered. Divide the scrambled eggs among the plates and quickly shave the truffle over the top—the paper-thin slices will melt with the heat of the egg.

SERVES 6

RESH BORLOTTI BEANS

STEPHANIE 🔊 With each visit to the market we became more familiar with the stall-holders. By our third week, at the herb stall they were tired of our students photographing their wares and tried to shoo us away. I was cross, too, as it had been a long morning and I wanted to buy some wild arugula. This was the very same stall where I had been given a bunch of wild cyclamen the week before. And then I watched a young man at the *borlotti* bean stall assist his elderly customer. She bought a lettuce ("smaller, please"), a carrot, two zucchini, and so on. Each transaction took some time, and throughout the young man was unfailingly helpful, tucking each purchase into the old lady's bag. At the end of it all, he assisted with extracting the correct notes and coins from her wallet. Gently, he pointed out that she had offered him a button, not a 500 *lire* coin, and then he settled her fine wool cardigan on her shoulders before each wished the other a good day.

THESE PAGES Scenes from the San Lorenzo *mercato*: two Florentine ladies exchanging the news of the day; fresh *borlotti* beans; towering stacks of crates.

> 2¼ pounds freshly shelled borlotti (cranberry) beans
> cold water
> ½ cup olive oil
> 1 fresh bay leaf
> 1 large sprig rosemary

Put the beans into a saucepan and cover generously with cold water, then add the remaining ingredients. Cook for about 45 minutes, then allow the beans to cool in the liquid. Serve as a side dish.

SERVES 6

COOKING LIQUID

Save the cooking liquid from the beans—it is delicious when used to deglaze a pan, added to a sauce (see the *sformato* on page 196), or as the base of a lovely bean soup.

BORLOTTI BEAN SOUP

Purée two-thirds of the cooked beans with their cooking liquid, then season to taste. Thin with water if necessary. Stir in the rest of the beans, a little sautéed garlic, if you like, and finish the soup with extra-virgin olive oil and chopped parsley and/or crumbled sage leaves that have been crisped in the oven.

GRILLED PIG'S KIDNEYS

The range of organ meats available at Florence's San Lorenzo market was quite remarkable. We had no trouble buying the snowy white caul fat needed for grilling kidneys or making our own version of *polpettine* (tiny sausages). Outside of Italy, you'll need to order caul fat from your butcher. Before use, soak the caul fat in lightly salted water overnight to remove all blood, then dry it thoroughly. It also freezes well.

> *1 extra-fresh pig's kidney per 4 people*
> *salt*
> *freshly ground black pepper*
> *2 fresh bay leaves per person*
> *caul fat*
> *sprigs of rosemary*

ABOVE The Tuscans love their pigs. The sty at the Bischi farm was filled with rubble in order to keep the pig's feet healthy and dry. It came complete with its own beautiful brick dwelling and the most magnificent views.

OPPOSITE Selling roasted chestnuts in the street market in Piazza del Mercato Centrale near San Lorenzo, Florence.

Remove the connective tissue from the kidney and discard. Salt the kidney liberally and allow it to rest for 1 hour, then rinse. Dry well with paper towels, then season with pepper. Slice the kidney thickly, then wrap each slice with a bay leaf in caul fat. Place the parcels on a grill over a moderately hot fire. The cooking time will differ according to the size of the parcel and the heat of the fire but you should allow about 5 minutes per parcel. Turn each parcel when the caul fat facing the fire has melted—this will be about halfway through the cooking. Allow to rest for 5 minutes before serving with *mostarda di Cremona*.

GRILLED CALF'S LIVER

Wild boar (*cinghiale*) sausage, grilled *polenta* with *gorgonzola* (see page 106), and this liver, grilled in a whole piece in our huge fireplace, made a great meal one night. We also added leftover Caramelized Onions (see page 194) to the liver as it rested.

> *1 pound 5 ounces calf's liver*
> *salt*
> *freshly ground black pepper*
> *Garlic Oil (see page 210)*
> *lemon juice*
> *extra-virgin olive oil*

Season the liver with salt and pepper, then brush it with garlic oil and grill over a hot fire, turning once or twice, for 15 minutes. Transfer the liver to a heated dish, then drizzle with lemon juice and extra-virgin olive oil and grind on more pepper. Rest for 15 minutes before slicing and serving.

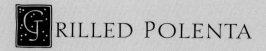

GRILLED POLENTA

MAGGIE ❧ Instead of cutting our *polenta* cake into wedges, as described here, we put the whole thing, dotted with *gorgonzola*, into a hinged grill for easy turning over the coals, and then cut it into wedges to serve. Stephanie and Tony turned the hinged grill over—and Elena came to the rescue when the *polenta* looked like it might end up in the coals!

While milk is not usually added to *polenta*, I find that it produces a wonderfully creamy, rich result.

> 4 cups milk
> 3 cups water
> 1 heaping teaspoon salt
> 2½ cups polenta (coarsely ground cornmeal)
> freshly ground black pepper
> ½ cup unsalted butter (optional)
> ⅔ cup freshly grated Parmigiano-Reggiano (optional)
> olive oil

In a heavy-based saucepan, bring the milk and water to a boil and add the salt. Gradually pour in the *polenta* in a slow stream, stirring continuously with a wooden spoon. Once all the *polenta* has been added, turn down the heat. Continue stirring so that a skin does not form. (Also, cooking the *polenta* slowly keeps it from becoming bitter.) The *polenta* will thicken and fall away from the sides of the pan. Remove the pan from the heat and season with pepper. Stir in the butter and cheese (this stage can be left out if you want the *polenta* to be less rich). Tip the *polenta* onto a large baking tray and pat it out with wet hands until it is ½-inch thick, then leave until completely cold.

Preheat a grill or broiler pan. Cut the *polenta* into the desired shapes and brush with olive oil. Put the oiled pieces of *polenta* onto the lightly greased cooking surface and leave them alone. *Polenta* releases itself from the surface once it has formed an adequate crust and can then be readily turned. Poking at it or trying to turn it too soon means that the forming crust will be left on the grill.

SERVES 6

GORGONZOLA

Instead of adding *Parmigiano-Reggiano* to the cooking *polenta*, cut the *polenta* into wedges, then dot each wedge with *gorgonzola* and return them to the fire or grill to heat through and melt the cheese.

RILLED RADICCHIO

Each time we went to the market, a different ingredient starred. On the last visit with our students, it was the turn of the deep-red *radicchio di Treviso*, a long-leafed specimen from the Veneto that was coming into its very short season. Some *radicchio* are loose-headed, such as the *radicchio di Treviso*, while others are a tight red ball (*di Chioggia*, for example). Some are variegated pink and cream, while others still are deep green with red splashes. Many are known by their local names, making it difficult to identify them outside the region, but what is pertinent is that they are either long or round.

Grilled *radicchio* is an acquired taste for some, as it is quite bitter. But if the platter of grilled morsels also includes rich things, such as pig's liver or kidneys (see page 104) and even chicken or *bistecca alla fiorentina* (see page 23), grilled *radicchio* provides a wonderful contrast. We found the *radicchio* in Italy to be exceptional—especially the *radicchio di Treviso*—and never found its bitterness overwhelming. We were tempted to use it for every meal!

radicchio
extra-virgin olive oil
good red-wine vinegar
1 clove garlic, finely crushed
freshly ground black pepper

Leave loose-headed *radicchio* intact at the root. If using a tight variety, cut it into quarters, leaving it attached at the root. Rinse the *radicchio* in water and then drain it in a colander. (If the *radicchio* is still damp as it hits the hot grill, the steam will in fact help rather than hinder the cooking.)

Mix 4 parts olive oil with 1 part red-wine vinegar, then add the garlic and pepper. Brush the outside leaves with this marinade and place the *radicchio* on a moderately hot grill over coals. Turn several times, basting it with the marinade. The grilled *radicchio* will have shrunk considerably and be browned and crisp on the outside but soft inside.

NEXT PAGE The Ponte alla Carraia (the "bridge of carts"), down river from the Ponte Vecchio on the River Arno, Florence. Originally built in 1220 to carry wool from merchants on the right bank to the dyers and weavers on the left, the bridge has been remodeled several times, including twice by Giotto, the father of the Renaissance, and most recently after the Second World War.

RILLED ONIONS

The marinade used when grilling *radicchio* (see above) can also be used with onions. Either halve onions horizontally or cut them into thick slices. (If halving the onions, there is no need to remove the skin—just slip it off after cooking.) If the cut onions are soaked in good-quality vinegar for 30 minutes before grilling, they will be less pungent. Brush the onions with the marinade and grill over a low-to-moderate fire (or toward the edge of the grill), turning and basting frequently. The onions will take a surprisingly long time (maybe more than 1 hour) and should be completely soft with caramelized edges.

L OST IS ALL THE

NOT SPENT

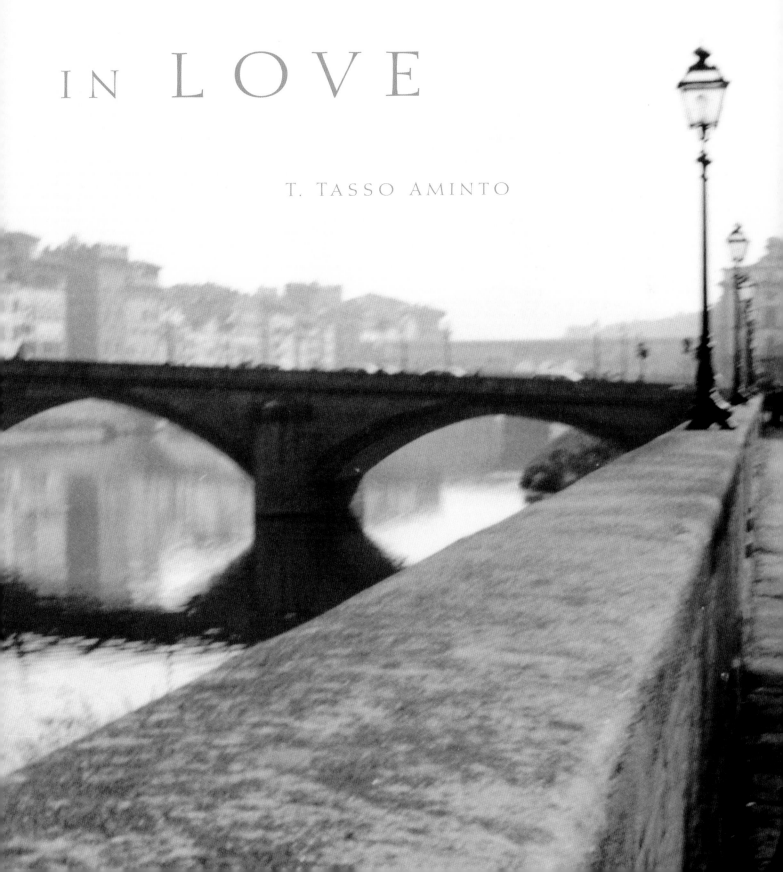

TIME
IN LOVE

T. TASSO AMINTO

SPINACH WITH LEMON, GARLIC, AND PINE NUTS

STEPHANIE 🌿 Toward the end of our time at the Villa di Corsano, I discovered that the huge trees that edged the gravel courtyard where we parked the cars were stone pines. Among the gravel could be found pine nuts, some still tightly encased in their very hard outer shell but most opened and the nuts eaten by the squirrels that seemed to be present in huge numbers. The squirrels were very cute, bright-eyed with dark silky tails.

At Cantinetta Antinori in Florence, we had this dish prepared with *cavolo nero*, the wonderful blue-green cabbage of Tuscany, and served on *crostini*.

2 cloves garlic, finely sliced
½ cup extra-virgin olive oil
6 handfuls small spinach leaves, stems removed
squeeze of lemon or orange juice
freshly ground black pepper
2 tablespoons toasted pine nuts or slivered almonds

ABOVE Who was this wild woman with the branch of lemons, we wondered of our merchant's fancy packaging?

Sauté the garlic in 2 tablespoons of the olive oil, then add the spinach and lift and stir until wilted. Drain the spinach well, then return it to the pan and add a good squeeze of lemon or orange juice, the remaining olive oil, and some pepper. Sprinkle on the nuts and serve.

SERVES 6

BROCCOLI RABE STEWED IN OIL WITH LEMON AND GARLIC

Broccoli rabe, or rape, known in Italy as *broccoletti di rape* or *rapini*, has a slightly nutty flavor and is delicious sautéed with garlic and olive oil, as spinach is. We served this as a side dish to grilled meats and on one occasion Maggie chopped blanched broccoli rabe quite small and stewed it as described below before adding four anchovies.

Wash 1⅓ pounds broccoli rabe very well, rejecting any old stalks or leaves in the process, then cut into 2-inch lengths. Blanch the broccoli rabe in a saucepan of boiling water, then drain. Squeeze out any excess moisture. Remove the zest from a lemon in ¾-inch wide strips. Gently stew the garlic in a little olive oil until golden, then add the drained broccoli rabe and the zest and cook until tender. Season with salt and pepper and serve.

GRILLED GARLIC

STEPHANIE ❧ Tony served each of us a whole head of grilled garlic alongside *bistecca alla fiorentina* (see page 23). He cut the top off each bulb with a sharp knife, just as one would a boiled egg, and the soft and sweet cloves popped out to be enjoyed with each mouthful. If you find this sweet garlic as irresistible as I do, it will become a necessary accompaniment to every barbecue. It is also great served with roast chicken, goat cheese, or sheep's milk cheese and crusty bread, or a selection of other grilled vegetables.

whole heads of garlic
extra-virgin olive oil

Blanch the garlic in boiling water for about 15 minutes or until a skewer slips easily through the skin. Drain and dry the garlic heads, then rub with olive oil and grill for 15–20 minutes until soft. To serve, cut in half or behead as described above.

ZUCCHINI WITH HOT BUTTER AND ANCHOVY SAUCE

STEPHANIE ❧ The range of zucchini in the markets was exciting—long, slender, deeply ridged fruit sat alongside small round specimens, some as tiny as a golf ball and others the size of a tennis ball. For one meal, I simply drizzled boiled tiny zucchini with extra-virgin olive oil. The slices had a slight viscosity due to all those just-picked essential juices, and the stem end was almost crunchy. The flavor was sensational.

6 small zucchini
¼ cup unsalted butter
6 anchovies, finely chopped
2 tablespoons coarsely chopped Italian (flat-leaved) parsley

Boil the zucchini for 5 minutes, then drain. Barely melt the butter in a saucepan, then stir in the anchovies and cook gently for 1–2 minutes. Slice the zucchini and arrange on a warm plate. Pour the hot sauce over the zucchini, then sprinkle with parsley and serve.

SERVES 2

PASTA

Maggie also used this as a base for a pasta dish by omitting the butter and instead tossing 17 ounces *ricotta* through the hot pasta along with a splash of extra-virgin olive oil.

TRIPE SALAD FROM LA FATTORIA AT TAVERNELLE

ABOVE For the last school session we bought bull's testicles from the organ meats stall—the butcher was delighted with our daring! They were poached for a few minutes, then the cooled slices were pan-fried in nut-brown butter, lemon juice, and pepper. Simon, Colin, and Tony abstained, as did Elena. But enough students tried them to win a wager for the cook. The verdict? A little like sweetbreads with an aftertaste of kidneys.

OPPOSITE At the Florence market we were given samples of succulent *prosciutto* and other delicacies on *crostini*. The stallholders never seemed disappointed if our sampling didn't translate into a sale.

STEPHANIE ❦ The tripe stalls at the San Lorenzo market fascinated everyone, as did the frilly shapes of unnamed parts and intestines and spleen and testicles, and something that was explained as being the milk glands of young heifers. Even for a lover of organ meats like Maggie it was a grisly and gristly spectacle at 10 o'clock in the morning.

After inspecting the tripe stalls, we had lunch at our regular market-day restaurant, La Fattoria at Tavernelle, where we'd asked them to prepare a tripe dish, since *trippa* is a Tuscan speciality. The whole meal, which included rabbit with wine grapes and *cartoccio* of *porcini* and *pancetta*, was good, but the tripe salad was the hit of the day, closely followed by a delicate *ricotta* sponge cake (see page 160).

At La Fattoria blanket tripe was cooked for 3–4 hours, implying that cleaned but uncooked tripe was used. Elsewhere, tripe is often sold prepared and requires much less time to cook. Choose either blanket or honeycomb tripe, which are the most tender.

> *tripe*
> *onion*
> *carrot*
> *bay leaf*
> *diced tomato*
> *finely sliced red onion*
> *finely sliced celery*
> *finely chopped red bell pepper*
> *finely chopped fennel bulb*
> *roughly chopped Italian (flat-leaved) parsley*
> *extra-virgin olive oil*
> *wine vinegar*
> *salt*
> *freshly ground black pepper*

Cook the tripe with onion, carrot, and a bay leaf for about 1 hour until tender. Drain the tripe, but retain some of the cooking liquid. Slice the tripe finely and toss it with diced tomato, a little red onion, and some celery, bell pepper, fennel, and parsley. Moisten the salad while still warm with a generous amount of olive oil, a spoonful of the reserved cooking liquid, and a few drops of wine vinegar. Check the seasoning and allow to cool. Serve at room temperature.

Octopus Braised with Tomato and Green Olives

STEPHANIE ✈ Maggie showed us how to deal with one of the monsters of the deep—octopus. Rosy-red and bronze, seared for a moment on each side over the fire, and then slowly simmered in a covered pan in extra-virgin olive oil, it was sliced and tossed with fresh tomato and olives and served with a side dish of fried whitebait.

If your tomatoes are not as small and perfect as those we bought from the market, it is best to peel them before removing the seeds.

4½ pounds octopus, cleaned and tenderized
½ cup extra-virgin olive oil
1½ pounds (4 medium) vine-ripened tomatoes, seeded and chopped
4 ounces (about 1 cup) large green olives
basil leaves, torn
salt
freshly ground black pepper
VINAIGRETTE
best-quality extra-virgin olive oil
juice of 1 lemon
freshly ground black pepper

Dry the octopus well with paper towels. Cut away the hard central beak and the anal portion. (If the octopus hasn't been cleaned, turn the body inside out and discard all internal organs and the ink sac.) Rinse and dry the octopus well (turn it right-side out if you've just cleaned it). Heat the olive oil in a deep, heavy-based wide saucepan until it just begins to smoke. Holding the tentacles, lower the head into the pan and seal the flesh. Lower the tentacles into the pan and seal for about 3 minutes, then lift out the octopus and repeat the process to seal the other side of the head and tentacles. When evenly sealed, cook the octopus, covered, over the lowest heat possible for 30–45 minutes until soft to the touch. (The cooking time will vary enormously, depending on how well the octopus has been tenderized. We have subsequently needed only 15 minutes' cooking time, but were using an exceptionally "tumbled" octopus.) Allow to cool in the juices.

Put the tomato and olives into a bowl, then drizzle with some of the oil used in the vinaigrette with some basil, salt, and pepper. Make a good quantity of vinaigrette to taste (don't add salt as the skin will supply this). When the octopus is cool enough to handle, slice it into the vinaigrette, then add this to the tomato and its dressing and mix well before serving.

BELOW First bash your octopus! If you cook octopus without tenderizing it first it will be as tough as old boots, so you must inquire when buying. Commercially, washing machines and cement mixers are used for this job. Even Peter's Italian broke down when he asked the fishmonger if the octopus had already been "bashed!" It felt very tight to us, so when we arrived back at the villa, there was nothing to do but use the front steps to tenderize it. The idea of wrapping the octopus in a dish towel didn't work, and in the end the only way was to hold it by the tentacles and go for it.

FISH STEW WITH SHELLFISH AND GREMOLATA

The names of the fish were meaningless to us, and we were completely at the mercy of the fishmonger. Once he understood the sort of dish we planned, he made the selection and we just smiled and indicated quantities! We bought *spigole o branzino, pagelli o fragolino,* and monkfish or *coda di rospo,* literally "tail of the toad" but also known as "chicken of the sea" because of its pearly-white flesh and firm texture.

ABOVE AND OPPOSITE As anyone who has shopped for fish in any European market knows, Americans and Australians are extraordinarily lucky. The high prices charged for fish in Europe reflect availability, now seriously affected by overfishing in many areas, as well as the premium the population is willing to pay for the best fish and shellfish. The same dish in America or Australia would cost approximately half what we paid in Italy.

4½ pounds mussels, scrubbed and bearded

1 cup white wine

20 thin slices baguette

1 clove garlic

olive oil

3 pounds blue-eye or snapper in 2-ounce pieces

3 pounds other firm, chunky fish, again in 2-ounce pieces

10 small calamari, cut into fine rings

BASE BROTH

2¼ pounds small fish, cleaned and chopped

2 fish heads, cleaned and chopped

1⅓ pounds fish frames, cleaned and chopped

¾ cup extra-virgin olive oil

1 bulb fennel, chopped

2 onions, chopped

2 sticks celery, chopped

6 cloves garlic, chopped

2 carrots, chopped

1 teaspoon fennel seeds

½ teaspoon powdered saffron

3 quarts Fish Brodo (see page 214) or water

4½ pounds ripe tomatoes, peeled, seeded, and roughly chopped

pinch of saffron threads

1 red chili

salt

freshly ground black pepper

GREMOLATA

freshly ground black pepper

½ cup freshly chopped Italian (flat-leaved) parsley

finely grated zest of 2 lemons

1 teaspoon finely chopped garlic

To make the base broth, briefly cook the fish, heads, and frames in ½ cup of the olive oil, then add the fennel, onion, celery, garlic, carrot, fennel seeds, and powdered saffron. Sauté for 5 minutes, then add the *brodo* or water. Simmer briskly for 20 minutes, then force the contents of the pan, bones and all, through the coarse disk of a food mill held over a bowl. Press on the residue in the food mill as hard as you can to extract maximum flavor from the bones.

Simmer the tomato in the remaining oil in another saucepan until cooked and most of the liquid has evaporated. Force the contents of the pan through the coarse disk of a food mill into the base broth. Transfer the broth to a saucepan, then add the saffron threads and whole chili and simmer for 10 minutes.

In another saucepan, heat the mussels with the white wine until opened. Strain the juices into the base broth and set the mussels aside. Taste the broth for salt and pepper, and if piquant enough, remove the chili.

Preheat the oven to 400°F. Rub the baguette slices with the cut clove of garlic, then brush them with a little olive oil and crisp in the oven for 5 minutes until golden.

Five minutes before serving, cook the fish in a wide pan in a single layer with just enough broth to cover. Do the same in another pan with the calamari, and reheat the mussels in another pan again. Make the *gremolata* by mixing the ingredients.

Divide the fish, seafood, and broth among hot, deep serving bowls, then scatter with *gremolata*. Encourage diners to break the garlicky toasts into the soup.

SERVES 10

ARDINES

The sardines we bought from fishmongers in Florence and Siena were always inexpensive and very fresh. We served deep-fried battered sardines alongside *risotto radicchio* made with fish *brodo* (see page 93), and enjoyed them wrapped in a grape leaf and grilled.

To prepare sardines, cut off the head, then slit the belly carefully and remove the guts. Open the fish out flat and ease out the backbone, snipping it with scissors to remove it. Rinse the sardine under cold water and rub off all the scales, then dry with paper towels and refrigerate until needed.

To cook sardines, dip them in batter (see page 143) and deep-fry, or coat them in seasoned flour or egg and breadcrumbs and pan-fry in olive oil and butter. Sardines cooked this way can also be stuffed with a simple paste of fresh breadcrumbs, grated lemon zest, and chopped parsley or fennel leaves, all moistened with an egg.

HOME AGAIN . . . .

THE PANIC OF UNLOADING . . .

WHERE TO PUT ALL THIS

FOOD!

The olive tree: the center of Tuscan life. Olive trees are planted in every landscape, whether as structured groves

or interplanted with the vines and grain that form the backbone of this region's cuisine. Even the very best wineries produce their own estate-bottled oils.

The
Olive
Grove

ELENA'S BREAD PUDDING

Because none of the team liked waste, Elena developed this dish to use up the sweet *cornetti* pastries leftover from breakfast. She served it sliced and warmed in the oven for breakfast, but it was also very good fried in a little butter, then sprinkled with cinnamon sugar and eaten with *mascarpone* or thick cream!

To make your own vanilla sugar, simply put a vanilla bean into a jar and fill it with sugar. The flavor and perfume of the bean will permeate the sugar quickly.

butter
3 cups milk
1¼ cups cream
6 eggs
½ cup vanilla sugar
2 drops pure vanilla (if using regular sugar)
¼ cup sherry (optional)
8 cornetti or croissants

Preheat the oven to 300°F and butter an 8-inch square cake pan well. Make a custard by bringing the milk and cream to a simmer in a heavy-based saucepan. Whisk the eggs with the sugar until foamy, then whisk in the warm milk and cream. Return the mixture to the rinsed-out pan with the vanilla (omit this if you've used vanilla sugar) and cook over a moderate heat, stirring constantly with a wooden spoon, until the mixture coats the back of the spoon. Stir in the sherry, if using, and strain the custard into a bowl.

Break the pastries into smallish pieces, then add them to the custard and allow to soak for 5 minutes. Pour the mixture into the prepared cake pan and stir slightly to ensure an even mix of pastry and custard. Place the pan in a bain-marie (water bath) and bake for about 1 hour or until firm to the touch. Allow to cool completely before cutting.

SERVES 8

ALAD CAPRESE

ABOVE AND OPPOSITE Everywhere in the San Lorenzo market in Florence there were green-shouldered tomatoes piled high and topped with signs declaring *pomodori insalata* or "salad tomatoes."

STEPHANIE 🦋 We who are often deprived of perfect tomatoes lust for those that are deeply red and sweet. But in Italy they were everywhere. The Italians (and Greeks) also appreciate the acidity, juiciness, and different sweetness to be found in ripe but not fully colored tomatoes. These green-shouldered tomatoes are favored for salad *caprese*, while the ripe, juicy red tomatoes are preferred for *bruschetta*, sauce, or preserving.

Chris Butler, Australian expatriate now with the *Movimento internazionale per la cultura dell'olio da olive*, spoke at each of our cooking school sessions about olive oil. He informed us that very few in the community are able to recognize basic and very common faults in much of the olive oil produced. We tasted olive oils under his guidance, including a very fruity Tuscan oil and a milder one, both without defect. To mark the difference we also tasted an oil bought that day from the supermarket and another unidentified but very bad oil. All were labeled "extra-virgin." Both the latter oils, we noted, were rancid and oxidized, and we also identified a "scalded" character in one of them. It is an interesting thought that most of us feel confident in recognizing rancid butter, milk that has gone off, or wine that is corked, and yet this other basic commodity is rarely rejected.

Select a great oil and you will understand why dishes such as salad *caprese* and *Panzanella* (see page 181) are celebrated. The oil contributes as much to the dish as do the fine-flavored tomatoes, balancing the acidity of the tomatoes and strength of the basil.

This salad should be prepared just before you serve it. If the cheese is as fresh as it ought to be, when left to stand it will ooze whey that will dilute the oil and spoil the look of the dish. The buffalo *mozzarella* at the Florence market was so fresh it was sold wrapped in strappy leaves to keep it firm and beautiful!

> 1 tablespoon tiny capers
> 6 basil leaves
> 4 ounces fresh buffalo mozzarella, sliced
> 4 green-shouldered tomatoes, sliced
> ¼ cup extra-virgin olive oil
> freshly ground black pepper
> salt

Rinse the capers in warm water and drain. Tear the basil leaves into 2–3 pieces each. Arrange the *mozzarella* and tomato on a platter, interspersing it with the torn basil. Season with the olive oil and pepper, and check for salt. Scatter the capers over the salad and serve.

SERVES 4

VITELLO TONNATO

The veal in the delicatessen section at the Florence market was the star. Firmly textured, rose-pink, and with a fine veil of silky fat over the loin, it was extraordinary.

There are many versions of this classic dish. It is ideal for a large gathering as it can easily be doubled and can also be prepared well in advance. The veal can rest in its sauce, undecorated, for 24 hours. Cover it with plastic wrap, however, to prevent the sauce from darkening too much. If you wish to keep the platter refrigerated for a day, reserve some sauce to add as a final coating before you decorate and present the dish. Allow 30 minutes for the dish to return to room temperature.

2 nuts (noix) of veal, each 1½ pounds, or 1 boned leg of veal in a net

4 anchovies, cut into pieces

1 onion, sliced

1 stick celery, sliced

1 carrot, sliced

3 cloves garlic

1 bay leaf

1 sprig rosemary

2 stalks Italian (flat-leaved) parsley

1½ lemons

½ cup dry white wine

water

extra anchovies

olives

capers or caperberries

SAUCE

1 × 6-ounce can tuna in olive oil, drained

1 tablespoon rinsed and drained capers

4 anchovies

1½ cups Mayonnaise (see page 212)

salt

white pepper

lemon juice (optional)

Make incisions all over the veal with the tip of a small knife and insert the pieces of anchovy. Select a large saucepan or enameled cast-iron casserole that will hold the meat fairly snugly. Put the meat, vegetables, garlic, and herbs into the pan, then add half a lemon cut in half. Add the wine and sufficient water to just cover the meat. Simmer very gently on the stove until the meat is easily pierced with a fine skewer. This will take 1½–2 hours. Allow the meat to cool in its strained cooking liquid, then refrigerate, preferably overnight or for up to 2 days.

To make the sauce, blend the tuna, capers, and anchovies to a smooth paste in a food processor, then add the mayonnaise. If the sauce is thicker than cream, thin it by adding a little veal cooking liquid. Adjust the seasoning—it may take a few drops of lemon juice.

Remove the veal from its cooking liquid and wipe it free of any jellied stock. Select a large meat platter and spread a thin layer of sauce on it. Slice the veal thinly and arrange a layer on the sauce, overlapping the slices a little. Cover with more sauce, then arrange more sliced meat, and more sauce. Continue until all the meat has been sliced and sauced, finishing with a layer of sauce. Thinly slice the remaining lemon and decorate the sauce, adding the extra anchovies, olives, and capers.

SERVES 6–8

LEFTOVERS

Any leftover sauce can be combined with the yolks of hardboiled eggs and used to stuff the whites in the celery heart salad on page 128 or as a simple dish in its own right. The cooking stock is also delicious when used as a base for a simple soup.

BELOW A summer's lunch of *vitello tonnato*, preceded by bread and fresh *ricotta* from the Bischi farm (see page 160) served with wild arugula and borage.

CELERY HEART, ROMAINE, AND OLIVE SALAD

OPPOSITE At the olive stall at the San Lorenzo market there were probably twenty-five different varieties available. We tried a new variety every time we visited the market.

This salad is a bright-green, leafy contrast to the creamy *Vitello Tonnato* on page 126. Any olives can be used here—black, green, some of each, mild or piquant. Sliced or whole baby radishes are also a good addition, as is sliced raw fennel.

This salad can also provide a base on which to build an elaborate luncheon platter. Imagine chunks of poached fish, just-opened mussels, warm boiled potatoes, and artichoke hearts, the whole creation drizzled evenly with wonderfully fruity new olive oil and maybe a dash of red-wine vinegar, or even a scattering of finely diced mild red onion.

> *2 bunches celery*
> *2 heads of romaine lettuce*
> *extra-virgin olive oil*
> *red-wine vinegar*
> *salt*
> *freshly ground black pepper*
> *6 hardboiled eggs*
> *½ cup black olives*
> *¼ cup freshly chopped Italian (flat-leaved) parsley*

Remove the outer stalks of the celery and reserve for use in another dish. Remove the outer leaves from the lettuce and reserve for another use (they can be used to make *Zuppa Pavese* on page 38) and put the inner leaves into a large salad bowl. Trim away any discolored parts from the celery hearts. Finely slice the inner leaves and the pale yellow leaves and put these into the bowl. Slice the solid section of each heart and add to the bowl, then toss.

Make a vinaigrette with the olive oil and vinegar, then season it and dress the salad, lifting and turning it with your hands to mix thoroughly. Shell the hardboiled eggs and slice them thickly. Arrange the salad on a large platter and dot with the egg and the olives, then scatter the parsley over it all.

SERVES 6

# CHEESE CROSTINI

Crostoni and *crostini* are slices of bread that have been either toasted under or on a grill, fried in olive oil or butter, or crisped in the oven. There is no limit to what can be served on these toasts. A little bit of yesterday's leftovers, perhaps bound with a well-made béchamel sauce, is often perfect.

When not in Tuscany, choose bread with a thinnish crust, such as a baguette, and cut it into ¼-inch thick slices.

12 slices baguette
olive oil or melted butter
1 cup freshly grated provolone
¼ cup freshly grated mozzarella
¼ cup freshly grated Parmigiano-Reggiano
¼ quantity Béchamel Sauce (see page 40)
1 egg yolk
salt
freshly ground black pepper

Preheat the oven to 400°F. Brush the baguette slices with olive oil or melted butter and toast them in the oven for 5 minutes or until a light golden brown.

Mix the cheeses into the béchamel sauce. Lightly whisk the egg yolk in another bowl, then stir into the cheese mixture. Check the seasoning. Spoon the mixture onto the toasted bread. Bake for about 5 minutes until the cheese is bubbling. Allow to cool for a few minutes before eating as the topping can be very hot.

MAKES 12

TOPPINGS

Consider toppings such as chicken livers (see page 46); sliced mushrooms that have been sautéed and mixed with fresh herbs; an olive paste made by processing olive flesh with capers, anchovies, and drops of lemon juice; or white bean purée (see page 173). Or wilt spinach with garlic, lemon juice, and extra-virgin olive oil (Tuscans would make this with *cavolo nero*, their black cabbage).

In Italy one can use

A WHOLE

Parmigiano-Reggiano

cheese as security against

a loan.

GRISSINI

BELOW Elena showed everyone how to make *grissini* and how to drag each little breadstick through olive oil and then fennel seeds before baking it.

OPPOSITE Grilled figs wrapped in *pancetta* with olives and *grissini*.

While we made *grissini* (Italian breadsticks) to partner the *Pinzimonio* on page 134, we also served it with the local *salame finocchiona* (a delicious, soft sausage flavored with fennel). We wrapped the sausage around the *grissini* and served them on an *antipasto* platter that included wrinkled black olives and white bean *crostini* (see page 173).

olive oil

finely chopped garlic

fennel seeds

salt

freshly ground black pepper

DOUGH

2¼ cups unbleached flour

1 teaspoon salt

2 teaspoons instant dried yeast

1 teaspoon honey

1 tablespoon olive oil

½ cup water

To make the dough, combine all the ingredients and knead well until smooth. Put the dough into a lightly greased bowl, then cover with a dish towel and allow to stand in a draft-free spot until the dough has doubled in size, about 1 hour. Punch down gently. Allow the dough to double in size again, about 30 minutes.

Meanwhile, preheat the oven to 350°F. Break off small pieces of dough the size of a walnut and roll each into a thin sausage about 10 inches long. Pour olive oil into a shallow tray, then add some garlic, fennel seeds, salt, and pepper and drag each *grissino* through this mixture. Space well apart on a floured cookie sheet and bake without delay for 15 minutes until browned and crisp.

MAKES 30

PINZIMONIO

MAGGIE ☙ Olive oil has long been important to me, but our nine weeks in Tuscany gave me a new love of this product. I now know that life is too short to use bad oil! Soon after our arrival, smelling and tasting olive oil, and taking notice of the incredible range of perfumes and flavors, became the first delight of a meal wherever we went.

Ann gave us a huge container of her own oil the day we arrived. It was the last of the year's, yet was still so fresh and "olivey" with a bite characteristic of Tuscan oils. But one great oil is just not enough: different dishes require different oils. The estate oil from each of the wineries we dealt with differed in complexity and character, one or two a little more mellow than I expected but wonderful for matching with more delicate flavors.

STEPHANIE ☙ *Pinzimonio* is the Italian version of the French *crudités*. *Pinzimonio* is always accompanied by a cruet of the finest extra-virgin olive oil and good-quality vinegar or lemon, a pepper grinder, and a saucer of sea salt. It always looks marvelous: celery with a plume of leaves attached sit alongside fennel bulbs, green onions, tiny zucchini, young artichoke hearts, tomatoes, and radishes, or almost any crisp vegetable that is good eaten raw. Blanched asparagus also makes an appearance. One dips and sprinkles and bites.

ABOVE The radishes we came across at the Florence market were perfect for *pinzimonio*—small, sweet, and not too "bitey" (i.e., peppery). We were also told by a very insistent stallholder that the round fennel bulbs were male and the longer, thinner ones were female, and that only the males were good enough to be used in *pinzimonio*!

We served the *pinzimonio* with Ann's own excellent fruity olive oil, which met with Chris Butler's approval. She also presented us with a bottle of her own red-wine vinegar that surpassed all others we tried.

CHARD AND GRAPES

On the first day of vintage, Elena harvested some of the tightly packed grapes from the villa's vines to stew with that leafy variety of beet, chard.

> *2 bunches chard*
> *salt*
> *2 tablespoons extra-virgin olive oil*
> *2 cloves garlic, finely sliced*
> *2½ cups (9 ounces) wine grapes, split and seeded, or seedless red table grapes*
> *freshly ground black pepper*

Strip the chard leaves from the stems. Roll the leaves and cut into julienne. Discard any stringy bits from the stems and cut into pieces about 2 x ½ inch. Bring a saucepan of lightly salted water to a boil and cook the stems for 2 minutes. Drain and squeeze well. Warm the olive oil and garlic over moderate heat, then cook the stems for 5 minutes, covered. Remove the lid and add the leaves and grapes and cook for another 5 minutes until the juices are syrupy. Check the seasoning. Serve with roast chicken.

SERVES 6

CORN-FED CHICKEN WITH POTATOES AND BAY

Once we sorted out the difference between a boiling hen and a roasting bird, we had some memorable meals. The roasting chickens were absolutely delicious: deep-breasted, yellow-tinged, full-flavored, and tender. Maybe yesterday they were scratching contentedly in the dirt just like their cousins we saw as we walked through the olive grove.

We served this chicken with chard stewed with wine grapes (see page 134) and spooned the stems, leaves, and grapes over the chicken on its platter.

ABOVE The chickens sold in the market came with head and feet intact; the shopper is in no doubt about the sex or age of their purchase. A different matter entirely from a supermarket chicken!

2 corn-fed chickens, each about 4 pounds
1 lemon, cut into 4 thick slices
2 fresh bay leaves
¼ cup extra-virgin olive oil
salt
freshly ground black pepper
6 large potatoes, quartered
12 large unpeeled cloves garlic
2 tablespoons verjuice (see page 219)
1 cup Chicken Brodo (see page 213)

Preheat the oven to 425°F. Cut up either side of the backbone of each chicken to remove it, then remove the wishbone, leaving the extra skin at the neck edge. Loosen the skin over the breast and work slices of lemon and half a bay leaf under the skin over each breast. Smooth the skin back into place and wipe the chicken dry. Rub 2 tablespoons of the oil seasoned with salt and pepper over each bird.

Dry the potatoes and roll them in the remaining oil with the unpeeled garlic cloves. Scatter the potatoes and garlic over the base of a large baking tray. Open out the chickens and settle them skin-side up over the potatoes, then roast for 40 minutes. Remove the tray from the oven and loosen the potatoes and garlic. Reduce the temperature to 400°F and return the tray to the oven for an additional 15 minutes. The chicken is done when the juices run clear when a thigh is pierced with a fine skewer. Remove the chicken to a heated platter and cover loosely with foil. (Transfer the potatoes to a fresh baking tray if additional crisping is required.)

Place the baking tray over heat and allow the juices to bubble hard, scraping any crispy and caramelized bits from the bottom. Add the verjuice and *brodo* and boil until you have a well-flavored sauce. Joint the chickens and return them to the platter with the potatoes and garlic. Check the seasoning of the sauce and spoon over the chicken.

SERVES 6

BAKED PRUNE PLUM AND MASCARPONE TART

OPPOSITE To counteract the problems the Italian butter caused when making pastry, Elena made a *pâte brisée* with egg white instead of water and had great success. She processed 2 cups all-purpose flour with ¾ cup butter and worked in 1½–2 ounces of egg white (one egg white is about 1 ounce), then rested the dough as in the recipe on this page before baking it blind.

The combination of crisp pastry, the rich, rich plums, and the fabulous Italian *mascarpone* (which was stiff, buttery, and low in acid) meant this tart was a triumph each time we made it. So simple! However, the unusual texture of the delicious Italian butter made pastry-making very perilous. The color of clotted cream, the butter was always very soft. We chilled the marble bench with bags of ice cubes and had to work very fast.

Other plum varieties, such as blood plums, can be used here with success. Especially nice are greengage plums, which make heavenly golden tarts.

> *2¼ pounds fresh prune plums (about 25)*
> *4 tablespoons unsalted butter*
> *2 cups mascarpone*
> *2 teaspoons plum brandy (optional)*
> SOUR CREAM PASTRY
> *1¾ cups + 1 tablespoon chilled unsalted butter, chopped*
> *2¼ cups all-purpose flour*
> *½ cup sour cream*

To make the pastry, pulse the butter and flour in a food processor until the mixture resembles breadcrumbs. Add the sour cream and pulse until the dough has just incorporated into a ball. Wrap the dough carefully in plastic wrap and refrigerate for 20 minutes.

Roll out the chilled pastry to line an 8-inch loose-bottomed flan pan. Chill the pastry crust for 20 minutes.

Preheat the oven to 400°F. Line the pastry crust with foil and then weight it with dried beans and blind-bake for 15 minutes. Remove the foil and beans and return the pastry crust to the oven for an additional 5 minutes. Allow the pastry crust to cool to room temperature and reset the oven to 410°F.

Halve and pit the plums. Arrange a layer of plums in a baking dish and dot with the butter. Bake for 20 minutes until cooked but still in shape, then allow to cool and reserve any juices.

Fill the pastry crust with the *mascarpone* (if it is very thick, thin it with the brandy) and top with the plums (display the golden interior of prune plums by having them cut-side up; blood plums can sit either way). Reduce any reserved juices to a syrup and drizzle over the tart. Serve immediately.

SERVES 8

THE HILLS, SO DEFINITELY

AT SUNSET

ETCHED AT MIDDAY,

so SOFTLY MODELLED . . .

EDITH WHARTON

ITALIAN BACKGROUNDS

To see a farmer making fresh *ricotta*, with his cows in the next stall and last year's onions and late-summer tomatoes hanging from the rafters alongside homemade *prosciutto*, is to understand self-sufficiency.

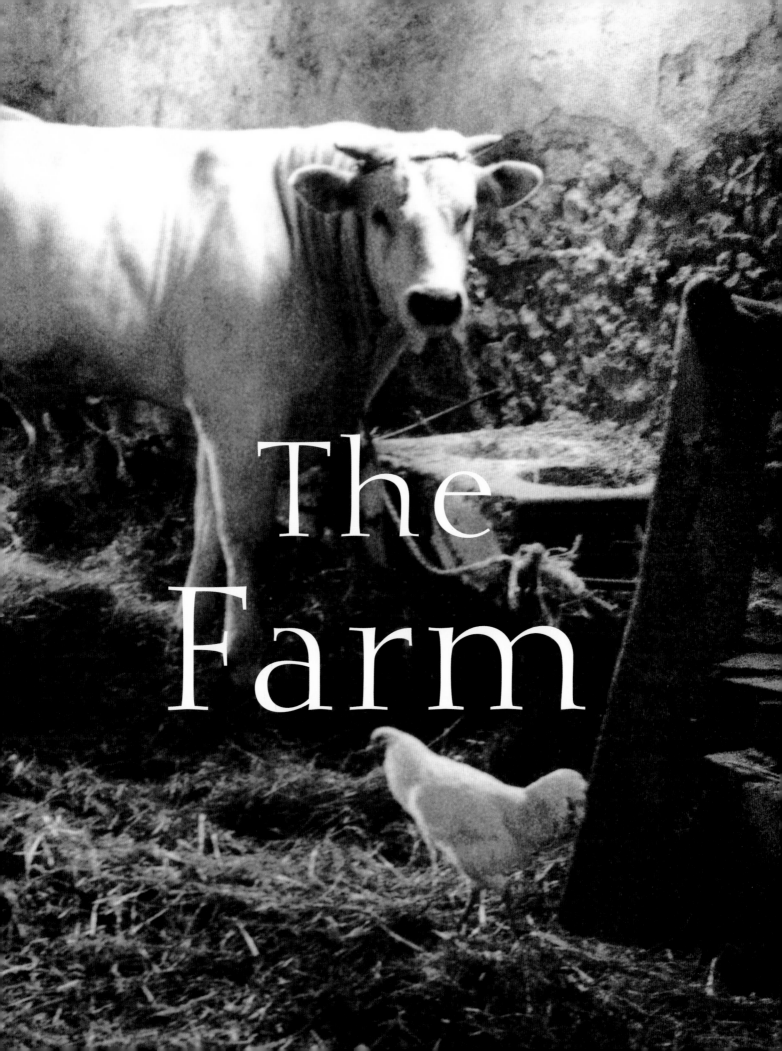

The
Farm

STUFFED ZUCCHINI FLOWERS

The dramatic male flower that grows on a long stalk from the center of the zucchini plant is best for stuffing (the female flowers produce the zucchini, so picking these too soon is a waste!). These gorgeous blooms are sold in bunches in Italian markets and are a very popular first course. They can be prepared in an elaborate way or be simply battered and pan- or deep-fried. In fact, when absolutely fresh there is no need for any stuffing.

Possible stuffings include finely chopped *bocconcini* tossed with chopped anchovies; finely diced *mortadella* sausage mixed with garlic, breadcrumbs, parsley, freshly grated *Parmigiano-Reggiano*, and drops of olive oil; or fresh *ricotta* or goat cheese mixed with chopped spinach or chard, and seasoned with salt, pepper, and nutmeg.

This batter is equally good for long, thin slices of tender zucchini or fresh sardines. We also enjoyed fried sage and anchovy "sandwiches" in a similar batter at the delightful Ristorante La Fattoria at Tavernelle.

ABOVE Preparing to stuff zucchini flowers. One Sunday night we found we had no *ricotta* or *mozzarella* in the villa, so we served zucchini flowers with an impromptu stuffing of eggplant and *Parmigiano-Reggiano*. On another occasion, zucchini blossoms and a mixed grill of *porcini* and *polenta* proved a great way to lead into a meal of rabbit, one of our favorites (see page 146).

OPPOSITE Huge piles of zucchini flowers were displayed in the markets only hours after picking.

olive oil
your chosen stuffing
12 zucchini flowers
BATTER
2¼ cups all-purpose flour
1 teaspoon salt
½ cup olive oil
1½ cups warm water
2 egg whites

To make the batter, put the flour and salt into a bowl and make a well in the center. Mix the olive oil with the warm water and pour into the flour. Work the batter until smooth, then leave it to rest for at least 1 hour. Beat the egg whites until stiff, then fold these into the batter. Use the batter immediately.

Pour olive oil into a large saucepan to a depth of 1½ inches and heat. The oil will be hot enough when a tiny cube of bread dropped into it browns immediately. Place a lump of your chosen stuffing in each flower and gently fold the petals around it. Dip the stuffed flower in the batter and then fry until golden brown. Drain very well on crumpled paper towels and serve immediately sprinkled with sea salt.

MAKES 12

Gnocchi with Sage and Burnt Butter

ABOVE One morning three of us walked to a medieval tower we could see in the distance. We passed banks spilling with wild cyclamen, crocus, and juniper bushes covered in ripe berries, and hedgerows overgrown with nettles. We saw old mill wheels and deserted stone houses, and walked alongside straggling vines. We picked wild arugula to serve with our *Vitello Tonnato* (see page 126), and found angelica growing near a church. We saw signs of digging in the earth. Had the spot held *porcini* or a truffle? Our imaginations raced but realistically it was far too dry in that part of Tuscany.

OPPOSITE Pillowy *gnocchi* with the simplest of sauces: crisped sage and burnt butter.

MAGGIE ❧ I have been making *gnocchi* at home for a long time, experimenting with recipes that use butter and those that use egg. I have found that the butter and kneading the dough make the *gnocchi* much lighter, but it wasn't until I made these *gnocchi* on the holiday in Umbria (the precursor to the whole Tuscan experience) that I realized that what makes more of a difference than anything else is the quality of the potato. In Italy there seemed to be two types, both waxy and yellow in color, but, sadly, they were sold unnamed. My favorite was the smaller, more deeply colored of the two.

> 1¾ cups all-purpose flour
> 1 pound 2 ounces waxy potatoes, peeled
> salt
> ¾ cup unsalted butter
> freshly ground black pepper
> 1 handful sage leaves
> extra-virgin olive oil
> freshly grated Parmigiano-Reggiano

Spread the flour out into a rectangle on your work surface. Steam the potatoes for about 15 minutes until cooked through. While hot, pass each potato through a potato ricer so that it falls evenly over the flour on the bench. Sprinkle the potato with salt.

Melt 2 tablespoons of the butter and drizzle it evenly over the potato. Using a pastry scraper, work the flour into the potato little by little until you have a firm dough. Knead the dough gently for 5–6 minutes (the timing is very important). Divide the dough into quarters and roll each piece to make a long, thin sausage about ½ inch in diameter. Cut each sausage into 1-inch lengths. Put a buttered serving dish into an oven set at about 300°F.

A large, heavy-based, 2½-inch deep baking tray is perfect for poaching *gnocchi*. Fill the tray with water, then salt it and bring it to a boil. When the water is boiling, raise the heat and quickly slip in all the *gnocchi* at once (if the tray is large enough to take the *gnocchi* in a single layer), then reduce the heat so the water isn't too turbulent. Allow the *gnocchi* to cook for 1 minute after they have risen to the surface, then skim them out and put them into the warm serving dish and season.

Cook the sage leaves in the remaining butter and a dash of olive oil over a medium heat until the butter is nut-brown and the sage crisp. It is important that the sage leaves become crisp without the butter turning black. Pour the butter and sage over the hot *gnocchi* and serve immediately as a first course with the *Parmigiano-Reggiano* on the table.

SERVES 8

RABBIT WITH ONIONS, PANCETTA, THYME, AND ROSEMARY

MAGGIE ❧ Rabbit is a great favorite in Tuscany. We had a fantastic rabbit dish at Ristorante La Fattoria at Tavernelle on our way back to Villa di Corsano from the market one day. The saddle had been boned and stuffed with the liver, some pork sausage, and lots of herbs, and then was roasted. It came sliced, with a sauce made with grapes from the restaurant's vineyard. The chef, who had preceded this dish with a tiny sage and lemon sorbet, had certainly used the ingredients in season!

The farmed rabbit we were able to buy from the Florence market was wonderful in quality, and the rabbits were a really good size. We cooked this dish a number of ways, each time following the three simple stages given below but altering the accompaniments. Once we served it with our favorite flat onions as well as truffled *polenta* bought in Greve on a day touring through Chianti; another time it was accompanied by fresh *borlotti* beans, and yet another rabbit meal featured *rapini*, flat onions, and *pancetta* cooked together.

2 farmed rabbits, each about 3½ pounds (including livers and kidneys)
3 sprigs thyme
1 sprig rosemary
olive oil
salt
freshly ground black pepper
verjuice (see page 219)
16 slices pancetta
24 pickling onions, peeled
1 cup Chicken Brodo (see page 213)

Remove the legs from the rabbits and set them aside, then remove and reserve the livers and kidneys. Strip all the sinew from the saddles. Strip the leaves from the thyme and rosemary sprigs and chop them. Rub the pieces of rabbit, including the livers and kidneys, with olive oil, salt, pepper, thyme, rosemary, and 1 tablespoon verjuice. Transfer the rabbit and organ meats to a tray and leave for 1 hour at room temperature.

Preheat the oven to 425°F. Cook the *pancetta* in a dry frying pan (or in the oven) until crisp, then drain on paper towels. Select a large baking tray that will hold the meat in a single layer without crowding. Roast the hind legs and onions for 15 minutes, turning them halfway through cooking, then remove from the oven and set aside. Cook the saddles for 10–12 minutes, turning halfway through the cooking, then set them aside. Cook the front legs for 6 minutes only, turning halfway, then set them aside to rest as well.

Transfer the baking tray to the stove over a moderate heat. Deglaze the tray with

½ cup verjuice and allow it to bubble up and reduce, then add the *brodo* and cook down to the desired consistency. Cover the baking tray loosely with foil and allow to rest in a warm place for 30 minutes.

Lightly sauté the livers and kidneys in a frying pan in a trace of olive oil. Divide each saddle into 4 pieces. Separate the muscles from the legs using your fingers and a sharp knife to free the meat from the bone where necessary. Heat the rabbit pieces in the juices in the oven for a couple of minutes, then toss with the onions and *pancetta* and arrange on a large serving platter. Serve with the livers and kidneys for an authentic feast.

SERVES 8

ROASTED ONIONS

If you cannot find pickling onions, try halving large, unpeeled onions. Put them into a greased baking tray and roast them uncovered in the oven at 425°F for 2 hours until well caramelized, soft, and collapsed. Discard the outer skin from the onions, then sprinkle with balsamic vinegar, extra-virgin olive oil, and freshly chopped parsley.

BELOW Our kitchen in the villa. The walls of the villa were decorated with beautiful hand-painted plates, most of which were at least a hundred years old and some much older. Their faded colors and chipped edges added to the sense of history. The presence of our photographer, Simon, added a new dimension to every meal. We dished up a portion for him to shoot on one of these beautiful plates and then served the students and ourselves.

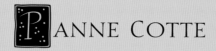

PANNE COTTE

STEPHANIE 🌿 This delicate cream is one of the most delicious desserts. I have flavored it previously with an oil of bitter almonds, crushed apricot kernels, rosewater, rose-scented geranium, ginger, and so on. But nothing too powerful that may detract from its pearly purity. Serve a delicate fruit sauce or poached fruit with a *panna cotta*—here we suggest Pot-roasted Quinces (see page 149).

sweet almond oil
1 package (¼ ounce) unflavored gelatin
1 cup milk
1 cup cream
¼ cup sugar
1 vanilla bean or crushed apricot kernel
few drops of pure vanilla or rosewater

Brush four 4-ounce (125 ml) pudding molds with the sweet almond oil. Gently heat the milk and cream in a saucepan with the sugar and vanilla bean (or crushed apricot kernel, if using), stirring until the sugar has dissolved. Gently pour the gelatin powder into the milk mixture, stirring to dissolve completely. Add the pure vanilla (or your chosen liquid flavoring), then strain the mixture and pour it into the prepared molds. Refrigerate for about 6 hours.

Run a knife around the edge to loosen each *panna cotta* and dip the base of the molds into hot water for 1 minute. Slip the desserts out onto serving plates. Serve with sliced pot-roasted quince and a little of the cooking juices, or your chosen fruit or sauce.

MAKES 4

MAGGIE'S POT-ROASTED QUINCES

STEPHANIE ❧ Maggie and I had a short but uplifting walk one afternoon. It was good to be out in the air and to watch the pickers in the vineyards tossing golden and blue-black grapes all into the one tub (the traditional way of making Chianti). We came across villas everywhere, many well hidden by clumps of trees. Vegetable plots held the last of the year's tomatoes and fruiting trees were featured in every garden. We picked a few bruised quince windfalls and then jumped guiltily as a rural police car drove past!

6 whole quinces, with stems and leaves, if possible
1½ quarts water
4 cups sugar
juice of 3 lemons

Rub the down from the quinces and wash them well. Pack the quinces tightly into a heavy-based saucepan with the water and sugar. Boil at a reasonably high temperature until a jelly starts to form, then reduce the heat to a simmer and cook for up to 5 hours. The quinces should be turned at least 4 times during cooking so that the deep-ruby color that they become goes right through to the core. Add the lemon juice in the last stages of cooking to cut the sweetness.

QUICK VERSION

If you don't have time to cook the quinces for hours, quarter the fruit first, then combine equal quantities of sugar and water and the peelings and cores in a saucepan (or add another quince or two). Stir this mixture over heat until the sugar has dissolved. Cook the quartered quinces in the syrup in a shallow, heavy-based pan on the stove or in the oven until softened, turning the fruit to ensure even cooking.

SERVES 12

ABOVE Preparing quinces for pot-roasting. After lunch one day, Elena packed the quinces and juices not eaten with the Caramel *Panne Cotte* (see page 150) into a small, round bowl. That evening, after the students had gone into Siena, we enjoyed a large Salad *Caprese* (see page 124), some *salami*, and the molded quince jelly, which was quite wonderful with our *gorgonzola dolce*.

CARAMEL PANNE COTTE

MAGGIE ❧ This alternative method of making *panne cotte*, which uses egg whites rather than gelatin as the setting agent, was taught to me by Stefano de Pieri from Mildura's Grand Hotel. He in turn had been taught the dish by Francesco, a chef who worked with him for a season. This splendid dessert was such a hit at Villa di Corsano that it was dubbed The Ultimate *Panna Cotta!*

> 4 cups heavy cream
> ¾ cup sugar
> 2 coffee beans
> ½ vanilla bean
> 10 egg whites
> pinch of salt
> CARAMEL
> 1 cup sugar
> ¼ cup water

To make the caramel, stir the sugar and water in a saucepan over heat until the sugar has dissolved. Stop stirring and cook until a deep-caramel color. Remove the caramel from the heat and immediately dip the base of the pan into cold water to stop the cooking. Pour the caramel into fifteen 4-ounce (125 ml) pudding molds, tilting to spread the caramel. Set aside.

Heat the cream in a saucepan with ½ cup of the sugar, the coffee beans, and the vanilla bean, stirring until the sugar has dissolved. Remove the pan from the heat and place over a bowl of ice or refrigerate until well chilled. Strain the cooled cream into a large bowl.

Preheat the oven to 350°F. Beat the egg whites with the salt until soft peaks form, then beat in the remaining sugar until just past soft peaks. Be careful not to overwhip the egg whites or they will not blend into the cooled cream. Stir a third of the egg whites into the cooled cream, then fold in the balance. Pour the mixture into the prepared molds, filling each as full as possible, then place these in a baking tray lined with a folded dish towel and pour in hot water to come three-quarters of the way up their sides. Cover the tray with foil and transfer it to the oven. Cook for 5 minutes, then turn the temperature down to 300°F and continue to cook for 1 hour 15 minutes—if the *panne cotte* are wobbly in the middle, give them another 15 minutes. Allow to cool, then refrigerate overnight to set the cream before serving. Slip a knife around the edge of each *panna cotta* and invert carefully onto serving plates.

MAKES 15

THE DISTANT PATCHWORK

NEXT TO ONE GROWING GREENLY,

OF A COMBED, NEWLY PLANTED FIELD

NEXT TO ONE LYING FALLOW

GRILLED EGGPLANT PICKLED WITH THYME, GARLIC, AND BALSAMIC VINEGAR

ABOVE AND OPPOSITE The Bischi farm. We first saw Signora Bischi knitting on the upstairs veranda of her house, a rustic building flanked by an arched stone wall. Barns stood on either side of the house; one included an archway in which a tractor sat, the old housing the new. Signora Bischi and her husband welcomed us on two separate occasions, selling us fresh *ricotta* and *pecorino* made from the milk from their own cows and sheep. Cows were tethered in a barn attached to the house, where we were also shown a "cool-room." Here we were offered a generous wedge of their own semisoft goat cheese.

STEPHANIE ❧ This delicious pickle formed part of an *antipasto* platter that included our own Preserved Mushrooms (see page 210) and fresh *ricotta* made only that morning.

Peter, Maggie, Tony, Elena, and I had gone in search of a farm selling goat cheese the week before. After driving along dusty tracks we came to the described isolated and ancient farmhouse. Outside was an old woman sitting with her knitting and a fly swatter. She seemed to be nearly crippled with arthritis and shouted at Peter. Yes, they did have some cheese, but it was not the best time of the year for it. She waved us inside, and we entered an interior that seemed not to have seen the twentieth century but for a few milk crates and the very old "cool-room" where the few cheeses were stored. Festoons of scarlet tomatoes still on the vine hung from the roof, as did giant *prosciutti*. There was the rich smell of livestock. After we had paid for our cheese there were smiles all around and she urged us to come back soon.

A week later, the other part of the group returned from a trip to the farm wild with excitement. They had been thrilled to see Signor Bischi making fresh *ricotta*. We ate it as the first course for lunch, still faintly warm, with borage flowers and arugula picked wild from the fields, and as part of the *antipasto* platter mentioned above for dinner that night.

1½ pounds eggplant
extra-virgin olive oil
6 cloves garlic, thinly sliced
¼ cup freshly chopped thyme (including stalks)
sea salt
freshly ground black pepper
¼ cup balsamic vinegar

Cut the eggplant lengthwise into ½-inch thick slices, then cut the slices in half diagonally. Brush with a little olive oil. Grill over coals or on a broiler pan under an overhead griller, turning once. Transfer the eggplant to a bowl or a deep baking tray and allow to cool a little. Sprinkle the eggplant with the garlic, thyme, salt, and pepper. Mix the balsamic vinegar with ½ cup extra-virgin olive oil. Pour two-thirds of this over the eggplant and turn to coat evenly, then leave to cool.

Pack the cooled eggplant into sterilized jars and pour over the rest of the vinaigrette. Shake the jars to release any pockets of air, then seal. This pickle is ready to eat straightaway but will also remain delicious for several months.

INESTRONE

STEPHANIE ❧ There are many, many varieties of *minestrone*. Some versions include short pasta, some include rice. In parts of Italy fresh herbs are added, and in others the soup is served at room temperature. In the south of France a very similar soup is called *soupe au pistou* and is finished with a generous dollop of *pistou* (borrowed from neighboring Genoa, where it is called, of course, *pesto*).

The best beans to use in a *minestrone* are fresh *borlotti* (cranberry) beans. These are sold in their speckled deep-pink and cream pods in late summer. If they are unobtainable fresh, they can be bought dried and soaked overnight. Dried *cannellini* beans can also be used. Weigh the soaked beans to match the weight of fresh beans required.

Rolled pieces of fresh pork rind are readily obtainable in Italian markets. Although not an everyday item elsewhere, pork rind can be ordered from a butcher. The rind can also be omitted, if you wish, or cured bacon or a pig's trotter may be substituted.

Italian cooks might also add the crust of a piece of good *Parmigiano-Reggiano* to the soup pot. An Italian friend of mine always adds such a crust when he cooks dried beans. I add it here as a reminder never to throw the crust of the cheese away. I keep mine in a capped jar covered with extra-virgin olive oil. The oil is used to drizzle in soups such as this or over dozens of other dishes.

Instead of Savoy cabbage, Tuscan cooks would use *cavolo nero*, the dark cabbage that gives *minestrone* its truly authentic flavor and color.

½ cup olive oil

1½ tablespoons butter

3 onions, finely chopped

3 cloves garlic, finely chopped

2 carrots, diced

2 sticks celery, diced

7 ounces pork rind, cut into 3 pieces (optional)

1 pound freshly shelled borlotti beans

rind from a piece of Parmigiano-Reggiano

1 cup tomato passata or 4 ripe tomatoes, peeled, seeded and finely chopped

6 cups Brodo (see page 213) or water

1 cup finely shredded Savoy cabbage

3 zucchini, diced

1 cup chopped green beans

sea salt

freshly ground black pepper

extra-virgin olive oil

freshly grated Parmigiano-Reggiano

Heat the olive oil and butter in a stockpot until the butter is foaming, then add the onion and garlic. Cook gently until the onion has softened. Add the carrot, celery, and pork rind and cook gently, turning the contents to coat all the vegetables. After an additional 5 minutes add the beans, cheese rind, tomato *passata,* and *brodo.* Cover the pot and cook at a gentle simmer for 1½ hours.

Add the cabbage, zucchini, and green beans and simmer for 30 minutes, then taste for seasoning. Discard the cheese crust before serving in wide soup bowls. Drizzle in extra-virgin olive oil and offer grated *Parmigiano-Reggiano* at the table.

SERVES 8

RIBOLLITA

Translating as "reboiled," *ribollita* is simply *minestrone* that has been reheated with bread added to it to stretch it a little further. A favorite supper at the villa, it was also enjoyed at Ristorante La Fattoria, where it replaced the summery cold tripe salad (see page 112) once the weather turned cooler. It was thick and burnished bronze with the distinctive color of *cavolo nero.*

OPPOSITE AND BELOW When we looked up on entering the building attached to the Bischi farmhouse we saw the previous season's bounty hanging from the rafters: burnished, crackling onions, beautiful tomatoes still on the vine, and *prosciutti* three times the size of a commercial one. We soon realized these were from their own huge white cattle, not pigs, hence their size!

CHOCOLATE TART

OPPOSITE Tony's arrangements complemented the villa's elegance and captured the essence of Tuscany. Sometimes they celebrated a special find in the market and were as simple as a huge platter piled high with deep-pink grapefruit. At other times Tony drew on the area around Villa di Corsano itself, bringing together such things as grasses, wildflowers, wine grapes, and windfall quinces.

Neither of us is known for our sweet tooth, but we found ourselves tempted a number of times in Italy by such delicacies as a bitter-orange mousse with pistachios, *affogato* (coffee and vanilla ice-creams drowned in freshly made espresso), and rice cakes and custard pastries we ate with coffee.

When we came to make this chocolate tart during cooking school, we couldn't find the bitter chocolate needed—anything else results in an overly sweet dessert.

7 ounces bittersweet couverture chocolate

¾ cup + 1 tablespoon unsalted butter

1 cup all-purpose flour

1¼ cups sugar

6 eggs

Preheat the oven to 350°F and line a 10-inch loose-bottomed flan pan with baking parchment. Melt the chocolate and butter in a bowl over a saucepan of simmering water, then stir until smooth. In an electric mixer, beat the flour, sugar, and eggs until very thick and pale. Mix the chocolate into the egg mixture at low speed. Pour the mixture carefully into the prepared flan tin and cook for 35–45 minutes. The tart will have a crusty top and will be fudgy in the middle. Cool completely before cutting.

SERVES 10–12

Ricotta Sponge Cake

We loved the *ricotta* cake they served to us at Ristorante La Fattoria the day we also enjoyed their tripe salad (see page 112). Simply a sponge cake split and filled with a very generous layer of *ricotta* mixed with yogurt and lightly sweetened whipped cream, it was dusted with powdered sugar and served with wild strawberries, red and black currants, and raspberries. We were also told that they sometimes add dried fruit reconstituted in brandy and water to the *ricotta* layer before the top half of the sponge cake is put in place; the cake is wrapped in foil and refrigerated for a couple of hours before being served with a dusting of powdered sugar.

> *1 cup fresh ricotta*
> *½ cup plain yogurt*
> *½ cup cream*
> *sugar*
> *1 sponge cake*
> *powdered sugar*

Whisk the *ricotta* until quite smooth, or blend it in a food processor, then mix in the yogurt. Whip the cream and sweeten to taste, then fold this into the *ricotta* mixture. Spread the mixture over the bottom half of a split sponge cake, then replace the top half. The *ricotta* layer should be a good 1–1½ inches thick. Dust with powdered sugar and serve with berries.

W ine is part of the Tuscan fabric, and every dwelling has its own vines, whether casually trellised or laid out in the smart, efficient rows of the modern viticulturist.

We tasted great wines in *enoteche* housed in medieval buildings, talked to vintners who embraced the best of old and new techniques, and stored our own wine in what was once an Etruscan building. Above all, we enjoyed wine as the Tuscans do, with great food.

The Vineyard

GOAT CHEESE IN GRAPPA

BELOW We enjoyed many Tuscan wines, including the Isole e Olena Cepparello on the left here. Made from Sangiovese grapes alone, it is referred to as a "Super Tuscan" and is made outside the rules laid down by the Denominazione di Origine Controllata (DOC), which monitors the production of such wines as Chianti Classico.

OPPOSITE Paolo de Marchi at Isole e Olena with grapes drying for *vin santo*, the luscious Tuscan dessert wine.

NEXT PAGE The view of the vineyards from Villa di Corsano.

STEPHANIE ❧ Paolo de Marchi, the charming owner/vintner from Isole e Olena who guided each of our groups of students through a tasting of his Chianti Classico, confirmed that almost all Italian winemakers also make their own *grappa*. This fiery brew is made from the must left after the winemaking process has finished, just as the French make *marc*. Our Italian male friends consumed it in copious quantities as a *digestivo* at the end of the luncheon party we held to thank all the "locals" who had helped us. They distinguished between *grappa* with a gentle, tamed character and, their preference, that which was more powerful and rustic. They set up a *grappa* tasting, but I contented myself with a *grappa* sniffing!

MAGGIE ❧ We organized the wine for the cooking schools with the help of Peter James from Negociants in Adelaide and included a case of *grappa*, thinking it a necessary part of the Italian experience, but even after all three cooking school sessions had finished we hadn't managed to make a dent in one of the 13-ounce bottles! The lunch for the "Italian connection" revealed all: it seems *grappa* is a tradition you need to grow up with, and that it takes a lifetime of acclimatizing to it. The *grappa* consumed on the day by our visitors had a lot less effect on them than the champagne had on the rest of us!

The strength of the *grappa* gives a wonderful balance to the creaminess of the goat cheese in this dish, and although you could substitute brandy, the "kick" of the *grappa* is hard to beat.

> 1 large clove garlic, finely sliced
> 2 tablespoons grappa
> ⅓ cup extra-virgin olive oil
> ⅓ cup roughly chopped Italian (flat-leaved) parsley
> freshly ground black pepper
> 13 ounces fresh goat cheese

Make a marinade by mixing the garlic, *grappa*, olive oil, parsley, and a few coarse grinds of pepper. Pour a little of the marinade into a glass or ceramic dish, then gently add the goat cheese and pour over the remaining marinade. Cover the dish with plastic wrap and refrigerate the cheese in the marinade for 24 hours, turning once or twice.

Serve the cheese, removed from the marinade, at room temperature with arugula dressed with extra-virgin olive oil and a good balsamic or aged red-wine vinegar. Slabs of bread, brushed with olive oil and toasted in the oven, are a must!

THIS YEAR, WITH ITS

RAIN, PROMISES

BRILLIANT SUMMER AND LIGHT

A VINTAGE TO REMEMBER.

MARINATED MUSSELS

The day Paolo de Marchi came to talk to us, we had a wonderful *antipasto* platter that included fried zucchini flowers stuffed with extra-fresh drained *mozzarella* mixed with chopped anchovy (see page 143), cuttlefish (see page 170), marinated sweet mussels, and small shrimp called *gamberetti*. Only one inch long, the *gamberetti* were boiled for just a minute and then were tossed with crushed fennel seeds, garlic, and parsley. These were eaten whole, just like soft-shelled crabs.

mussels, bearded and cleaned
finely chopped onion
parsley stalks
white wine
extra-virgin olive oil
cider vinegar
very finely chopped shallots
lots of coarsely chopped Italian (flat-leaved) parsley

ABOVE Paolo de Marchi in the barrel room at Isole e Olena. He charmed us all, not only because of his lucid explanation of the old and new viticultural traditions in Chianti and his assessment of the region's future directions, but because of his personal warmth.

OPPOSITE A close-up view of some *vin santo* grapes drying on racks. The grapes stay on the racks for several months (see page 178).

Place the scrubbed, unopened mussels no more than 2 layers deep in a wide pan (a wok is good). Scatter some chopped onion and parsley stalks over the mussels, then pour in white wine to a depth of ½ inch. Jam on the lid and turn the heat to maximum. In 4–5 minutes there will be a great gush of steam from the pan and, when the lid is removed, you will see that the shells have sprung apart. Using tongs, transfer the opened mussels to a dish, then return any unopened ones to the heat for another minute or so. Add the opened mussels to the dish and discard any that are still closed. Strain sufficient cooking juices over the mussels so that they stay moist as they cool a little before adding the dressing.

Mix 4 parts olive oil with 1 part cider vinegar and add the remaining ingredients—make sure there is enough parsley to make a thick dressing. Marinate the mussels for 30 minutes before serving.

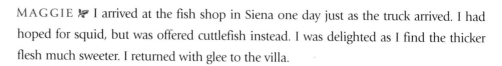

CUTTLEFISH SALAD

OPPOSITE Peter sampling the 1993 Brunello di Montalcino, one of the greats. The medieval town of Montalcino is famed for its big, dry red wine made from a clone of the Sangiovese grape that has adapted particularly well to the area. By law Brunello di Montalcino must be aged in the barrel for a minimum of three years and is sold after a total of four years' aging.

BELOW Paolo de Marchi kept us well entertained in the barrel room at Isole e Olena.

MAGGIE ❧ I arrived at the fish shop in Siena one day just as the truck arrived. I had hoped for squid, but was offered cuttlefish instead. I was delighted as I find the thicker flesh much sweeter. I returned with glee to the villa.

¼ cup currants

2 tablespoons red-wine vinegar

6 cuttlefish, cleaned (squid may be substituted)

2 tablespoons extra-virgin olive oil

1 red onion, thinly sliced

1 cup dry white wine

3 tomatoes, peeled, seeded, and chopped

1 handful black olives

¼ cup freshly chopped Italian (flat-leaved) parsley

2 tablespoons toasted pine nuts

Preheat the oven to 350°F. Soak the currants in the red-wine vinegar for 30 minutes, then drain. Meanwhile, remove the tentacles from the cuttlefish bodies and set them aside. Cut the bodies into pieces about 2 x 2 inches and transfer them to an ovenproof dish. Add the olive oil, onion, wine, and tomato to the dish and cook, covered, in the oven for 1 hour. Check if the cuttlefish is tender by piercing it with the tip of a knife (the flesh should not offer any resistance)—if not, cook for an additional 15 minutes. Add the tentacles and olives and cook for another 15 minutes, then stir in the parsley, pine nuts, and reconstituted currants and season with pepper. Serve at room temperature as part of an *antipasto* platter.

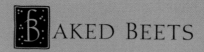AKED BEETS

For one meal we preceded the *Rotolo di Spinaci* (see page 174) with a vegetarian *antipasti* that included baby zucchini that had been boiled for 5 minutes, quartered, and then drizzled with extra-virgin olive oil and sprinkled with sea salt, pepper, and freshly chopped parsley. Green beans were added to a dish of stewed artichokes (see page 72), and the last of the Caramelized Onions (see page 194) were tossed through to make a salad. Zucchini flowers were gently sautéed in butter and olive oil and then sliced through their middles. Freshly grilled eggplant and red bell pepper and our own pickled mushrooms (see page 210) topped off this wonderful feast.

When planning this meal back home, we had decided to serve baked beets as part of the vegetarian *antipasto*, but to our surprise nowhere did we find raw beets. Even at the San Lorenzo market in Florence the only beets we saw were already cooked. This seemed doubly strange since the very young beet tops were readily available to sauté with olive oil and maybe browned breadcrumbs as a sauce for pasta.

baby beets, tops trimmed back to 1 inch
extra-virgin olive oil
1 tablespoon water
sprigs of thyme
red-wine or balsamic vinegar
mustard
freshly ground black pepper

Preheat the oven to 425°F. Pack the beets into a stainless steel or enameled baking dish just large enough to hold a single layer and drizzle over extra-virgin olive oil, then add the water and tuck in a sprig or two of thyme. Cover the dish with foil and bake for 40–60 minutes. The beets are ready when a skewer can be inserted easily. These beets can be served in their skins or peeled.

WARM SALAD

For a warm salad, toss diced baked beets with roasted garlic cloves, anchovies that have been soaked in milk for 10 minutes, and a vinaigrette of red-wine vinegar, orange juice, and extra-virgin olive oil. For a different flavor contrast, add pink grapefruit or orange segments, sautéed beet leaves, and toasted walnuts to tiny whole baked beets.

WHITE BEAN PURÉE

One of the most characteristic things about Tuscan cooking is its use of readily available and simple ingredients: grapes, red wine, tomatoes, olive oil, bread, and, of course, beans. Even pheasant and wild boar, which sound exotic to us, fall into this group.

We tasted bean soups, stews, salads, and purées such as this one at various meals. Bean purées can be made more or less sloppy depending on whether the final result is to be a soup, served hot or cold with a drizzle of extra-virgin olive oil, or, as here, to be thick enough to be spread on bread before being placed under the broiler.

6 ounces dried cannellini beans, soaked overnight

3 cups cold water

1 tablespoon tomato paste

salt

1 teaspoon freshly chopped garlic

1 teaspoon finely chopped fresh rosemary

extra-virgin olive oil

¾ cup hot Brodo (see page 213)

juice of ½ lemon

freshly ground black pepper

Rinse the soaked beans, then put them in a large saucepan with the water and add the tomato paste and a scant pinch of salt. Bring to a boil, then lower the heat and simmer, uncovered, for 2 hours. The beans should be covered with water for the first 1½ hours. When the beans are tender almost all the water should have been absorbed. Purée in a food processor.

Sauté the garlic and rosemary in a little olive oil. Add the purée and mix well. Pour in the hot stock and stir over heat until thoroughly absorbed. The purée should now be smooth, thick, and shiny. Add extra oil, lemon juice, salt, and pepper to taste. Serve the purée on toasted, dense bread and warm in the oven for 10 minutes or place under the broiler until golden, if desired.

The purée keeps well, refrigerated in a covered container, for several days.

ROTOLO DI SPINACI

OPPOSITE *Rotolo di Spinaci*, pictured here with burnt butter, crisped sage leaves, and freshly shaved *Parmigiano-Reggiano*.

MAGGIE ❦ *Rotolo* became a favorite dish among our students, as well as the friends and family who joined us on holidays after the cooking school.

The method for making the pasta includes using a food processor initially, unlike the fresh egg pasta dough on page 211, which is made by hand to ensure a shiny result. (You will find that you will have leftover pasta—this will cover any mishaps. Any remains can be frozen or used to make *ravioli*.) We were particularly pleased with ourselves the day we used up all the egg yolks left over from making *panne cotte*—for the 4½ cups flour we used 12 yolks and 1½ egg whites. The resulting pasta was rich and beautifully gold!

The first time we made this dish in the cooking school we realized we'd forgotten to buy cultivated mushrooms at the market the day before. There was nothing else to do— we just had to make it with fresh *porcini*! The small *porcini* destined to be wrapped in grape leaves and grilled for the *antipasto* platter were commandeered, and instead of being a good, rustic meal, the *rotolo* became a dream dish.

I reconstituted and then cooked the dried *porcini* as in the method below. The fresh *porcini* were pan-fried in butter with a little chopped garlic until caramelized, and the pan was deglazed with some of the juices from the soaking mushrooms, which reduced to a syrup. (The leftover juices were set aside for the *sformato* that appeared in the banquet on the final night of the school—see page 196.) The flavor was fabulous.

On another occasion, we found that the twist in the pasta hadn't cooked through after the usual poaching time, so, under the direction of Elena, we unwrapped the parcels and finished off the cooking in a pan of lots of melted butter. A pitcher of nut-brown butter and a plate of crisped sage leaves were at the ready to finish off the dish, and I carved with great success at the table.

While a traditional dish, this recipe is based on one in *The Café Cookbook: Italian Recipes from London's River Café* by Rose Gray and Ruth Rogers.

ABOVE Feeding the pasta sheet through the pasta machine.

BELOW Arranging the spinach and mushroom fillings over the finished pasta sheet.

PASTA DOUGH

4⅓ cups unbleached all-purpose flour

1 teaspoon sea salt

4 large eggs

6 large egg yolks

semolina flour

FILLING

verjuice (see page 219)

1½ ounces dried porcini

2 tablespoons butter

1 red onion, finely chopped

1 tablespoon fresh oregano

1¾ pounds fresh spinach, washed, blanched and chopped

zest of 1 lemon

sea salt

freshly ground black pepper

1½ tablespoons olive oil

2 cloves garlic, chopped

9 ounces field mushrooms, coarsely sliced

12 ounces ricotta

½ cup freshly grated Parmigiano-Reggiano

freshly grated nutmeg

To make the pasta dough, put the flour and salt into a food processor and add the eggs and egg yolks. Pulse until the pasta begins to come together into a loose ball of dough. Knead the pasta dough on a work surface dusted with semolina flour until smooth, about 3 minutes.

Divide the dough into quarters (if you plan to roll it by hand, divide it in two—see the note at the foot of the next page) and briefly knead each piece into a ball. Wrap the dough in plastic wrap and refrigerate for at least 20 minutes and up to 2 hours.

Meanwhile, make the filling. Warm some verjuice in a saucepan, then use this to reconstitute the dried *porcini*—they will take 15–20 minutes. Heat the butter in a frying pan and cook the onion until softened, then add the oregano, spinach, and lemon zest. Stir to combine, then season and allow to cool.

Drain the *porcini* and reserve the strained soaking liquid. Wash the *porcini* to remove any grit. Heat the olive oil in a frying pan and gently cook the garlic for a few minutes. Add the field mushrooms and cook, stirring, over a high heat for 5 minutes. Add the *porcini* and cook gently for 20 minutes, adding a little of their strained soaking liquid from time to time to keep the mushrooms moist. Use all the soaking liquid—you may need to turn up the heat to evaporate the remaining juices. Season and allow to cool. When cold, chop roughly.

Put the *ricotta* into a large bowl and break it up lightly with a fork, then add the spinach mixture, the *Parmigiano-Reggiano* and a generous amount of nutmeg. Add salt and pepper, if necessary, and set aside.

Using a pasta machine, put a piece of pasta dough through the maximum aperture 8–10 times until shiny and silky, each time folding one end into the center and the other over this, then giving the dough a turn to the right before rolling it again. Once this has been done, put the dough through the other settings until you reach the second-to-last or finest setting. It does not matter if there are a few holes or tears—these are easily patched. You should have a pasta sheet about 4 x 12 inches by this time. Repeat this process with the remaining three pieces of dough. Join two sheets of pasta together at the longest edge, brushing the edges with water to seal, to make a sheet about 8 x 12 inches. Repeat this with the other two sheets of pasta, then trim the edges to straighten them.

Transfer each sheet of pasta to a large, clean dish towel—choose one that is as smooth as possible as any texture will leave a pattern—and position it so that the longer edge is facing you. Spoon the mushroom mixture in a line about 2 inches wide along the edge of the pasta nearest to you. Cover the rest of the pasta with the spinach and *ricotta* mixture to a thickness of about ¼ inch. Starting with the mushroom edge, gently roll up the pasta into a log 2½ inches in diameter and 12 inches long, working away from you and using the dish towel to help guide you (see photograph at right). Wrap the *rotolo* in the cloth as tightly as you can, folding the ends in to secure the parcel and tying it with string to hold it in shape and keep the water out during cooking (see photograph). Repeat this process with the remaining pasta sheet and filling.

Bring a fish kettle or large, deep baking tray of salted water to a boil. Carefully slip in a wrapped *rotolo*, making sure it's submerged, then cover and simmer for 18–20 minutes. Remove the *rotolo* and allow to rest while cooking the second. Unwrap the *rotoli*, then transfer them to a board and cut into 2-inch-thick slices. Serve two slices per person and offer grated *Parmigiano-Reggiano* at the table.

SERVES 8–10

BY HAND

You can also roll the pasta by hand, although it is fairly difficult. In this case, divide the dough in two rather than into quarters before resting it. Dust a work surface with semolina flour and roll the dough until it is as thin as possible. The work area should be quite cool so that the pasta does not dry out.

ABOVE Rolling the *rotolo* with the help of a dish towel.

BELOW The carefully trussed *rotoli* poaching in a baking tray (our large trays were able to take more than one roll at a time).

CHOCOLATE SLAB WITH ALMONDS

OPPOSITE The entrance to Paolo de Marchi's vineyard and winery, Isole e Olena in Chianti. The vineyard was opposite these gates, tucked into the side of the hill, and surrounded by dense forest. On seeing this, Paolo's stories of the *cinghiale* (wild boar) coming out of the woods to eat the grapes the night before vintage seemed all too possible. Marta de Marchi believes that the flavor of *cinghiale* has become much milder since these animals started preferring well-cared-for Chianti grapes to their usual food.

STEPHANIE ❧ We enjoyed this delicious treat along with our own candied ruby grapefruit peel (see page 69) and Maggie's quince paste on more than a few occasions with *vin santo*, the luscious Tuscan dessert wine.

Making *vin santo* is a labor of love. The grapes are dried for months after harvesting until they are finally pressed to yield a very small amount of rich, raisiny juice. At this point the previous vintage is drained from its lees in the barrel and bottled and the new wine is added. It remains in the barrel for an additional four years. Alcohol is added to many inferior wines, and these are labeled *vino liquoroso* rather than *vino da tavola*, which signifies authentic *vin santo*. Inferior wines can taste raw rather than mellow and are often cloudy, unlike the golden wines we enjoyed.

bittersweet couverture chocolate
blanched almonds
sweet almond oil or olive oil

Preheat the oven to 350°F and line a baking tray with baking parchment. Bring a saucepan of water to a full boil, then turn the heat down very low. Break the chocolate into pieces and put it into a bowl wide enough to be suspended by the saucepan and place it over the hot water. Cover tightly with a lid, plastic wrap, or foil, so that neither water nor steam will spoil the chocolate (a drop of moisture will cause the chocolate to seize). Allow the chocolate to melt slowly.

While the chocolate is melting, roast the almonds in the oven for 5–10 minutes until a deep gold. Chop very roughly. Remove the bowl from the saucepan, then remove its lid or covering. Tip the almonds into the melted chocolate and stir very briefly.

Brush the lined baking tray with sweet almond oil or a trace of olive oil. Tip the chocolate mixture onto the tray, tilting to spread it into a thin layer. Allow to set. Break into irregularly shaped pieces and store in a cool place.

PANZANELLA

STEPHANIE ❧ I ordered *panzanella* at Ristorante Nello La Taverna in Siena to see how a true Tuscan put it together. I was pleased to find that, with more crumbling of the bread, my version was fine. This restaurant was quite exceptional—we particularly enjoyed fresh anchovies, marinated in extra-virgin olive oil, with shaved white truffles, and a torte of chickpeas and fresh artichokes. The owner told us of his philosophy regarding produce, of letting ingredients speak for themselves, of respecting the traditions of his region, and yet allowing room for a personal interpretation. He did not know that he was preaching to the converted.

Panzanella is a traditional Tuscan dish that can be expanded easily and relies on good bread, good oil, and the ripest vegetables for its flavor. Elizabeth Romer records in her book *The Tuscan Year* that in some parts of Tuscany before the tomatoes ripen *panzanella* can simply be bread, olive oil, onion, and perhaps green garlic.

OPPOSITE A detail from one of the frescoes in the salon at Villa di Corsano.

2 thick slices coarse bread at least a day old

cold water

6 ripe tomatoes, cubed

1 small red onion, finely diced or very thinly sliced

½ cucumber, diced

1 stick celery, finely sliced

2 cloves garlic, crushed

½ cup basil leaves, torn into small pieces

⅓ cup extra-virgin olive oil

2 tablespoons red-wine vinegar

salt

freshly ground black pepper

Remove the crusts and cut or tear the bread into small pieces. Put the bread into a bowl and sprinkle with cold water. The bread should be moist but not soggy. Add the vegetables, garlic, and basil. Dress with the olive oil and vinegar, then toss well and adjust the seasoning. Allow to stand for 30 minutes, so that the flavors blend.

SERVES 4

RAVIOLI OF MELANZANE

ABOVE An old bottle hanging in the entrance hall at the Bischi farm.

BELOW Antique wooden ravioli and spaghetti cutters bought in Florence.

STEPHANIE ❧ I had exquisite *ravioli* on a number of occasions when eating out in Italy. At the Ristorante Nello La Taverna in Siena I had delicious eggplant (*melanzane*) *ravioli* much like this recipe, although it came with a sauce of melted zucchini flowers. But it was at the Taverna e Fattoria dei Barbi del Casato, a working farm-cum-restaurant a handful of miles from the wine town of Montalcino, that I had the very finest *ravioli* I can ever remember eating. Once again it must be said that the quality of the ingredients in Italy determines whether something is memorable or ordinary. This simple dish of spinach-and-*ricotta* filled *ravioli* was sheer poetry. The *ravioli* were quite large—four to a serving. The pasta was strong and yet tender, bright yellow, and full of the flavor that comes from country eggs. The *ricotta* was as light as whipped cream, its texture at once creamy and firm. Not a suspicion of whey or graininess. Just puffed pillows of delectable filling sauced with browned butter and sage.

The farm made its own cheese, both the *ricotta* mentioned and *pecorino*, its own oil and wine, and produced the pigs used for the homemade *salami* and pork. They also claimed to produce the charcoal used for the grilling fire!

Ricotta comes two ways. Freshly made and dripping, epitomized by the warm *ricotta* from the Bischi farm pictured on page 161, is the best of all, but it needs to be drained overnight in a muslin-lined sieve before being used in cooking. The firm product available from most supermarkets does not need draining.

We were in Italy at the height of the eggplant season, so the plump, shiny fruit we were using were small to medium. These did not need salting, but larger specimens, which have larger seeds, are likely to be bitter and therefore need to be salted.

The pasta dough needed to make *ravioli* must be fine and soft. The dough used to make the *rotolo di spinaci* on page 174 is perfect. This recipe makes 4 very large *ravioli*—only one per person is required.

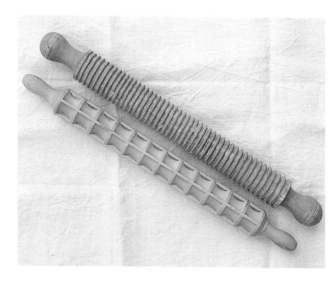

12 ounces eggplant

olive oil

2 tablespoons rinsed and drained tiny capers

1½ cloves garlic, finely chopped

½ cup freshly chopped basil

juice of 1 lemon

sea salt

freshly ground black pepper

3½ ounces goat cheese or 7 ounces ricotta, drained overnight

1 quantity pasta dough (see page 176)

best-quality extra-virgin olive oil

freshly grated Parmigiano-Reggiano

Slice the eggplant, then salt it if large and leave to drain for 30 minutes. Rinse the eggplant and pat it dry with paper towels, then peel and dice it finely. Pour olive oil into a frying pan to a depth of 1 inch, then fry the eggplant until golden, turning it regularly. Remove the eggplant with a slotted spoon and allow it to drain on paper towels. Put the drained eggplant into a bowl.

In a separate pan, sauté the capers in a little olive oil, then add these to the eggplant. Sauté the garlic in the same oil until translucent but not golden, then add to the bowl. Tip the basil into the bowl with the lemon juice, then season. Carefully fold in the goat cheese or *ricotta* and check the seasoning again. Allow the mixture to sit for a while for the flavors to meld.

Make the pasta dough as instructed, dividing it in two before allowing it to rest. Using a pasta machine, roll each piece of dough through the settings until you reach the finest. Trim the ends of the pasta sheets to square them up, ensuring the sheets are the same length. Lie the sheets on a floured work surface, then place 4 spoonfuls of filling about 3 inches apart down one of these. Flatten out the filling a little. Moisten the pasta around the filling with a pastry brush dipped in water. Carefully position the remaining sheet of pasta over the other, pressing down around the mounds of filling to ensure a good seal. Cut between each mound of filling to create 4 large *ravioli*.

Bring a shallow pan of water to a boil, then add salt and reduce to a simmer. Slide in two large *ravioli* at a time—they will rise to the surface very quickly and will only take two minutes to cook. Drain the *ravioli* well, then drizzle with extra-virgin olive oil (a green Tuscan oil, if possible), add *Parmigiano-Reggiano,* and serve. (These *ravioli* are also delicious served with nut-brown butter and crisped sage.)

SERVES 4

GRILLED LEG OF LAMB WITH ROSEMARY AND GARLIC

MAGGIE 🍐 The legs of lamb we found in the Florence market and at our local butcher were quite tiny. Tony grilled the boned meat to perfection over the coals in our much-loved kitchen fireplace—the meat was charred on the outside but pink and moist in the middle. At the last moment we thought of melting some of my quince paste and basting the cooking meat with it—delicious.

The lamb joined grilled and sliced wild boar sausages, calf's liver cooked as a whole piece (see page 104), and *polenta* grilled as a cake and dotted with *gorgonzola* (see page 106) to make yet another fantastic feast from the fire. The grilling days were my favorites.

> *olive oil*
> *juice of 1 lemon*
> *salt*
> *freshly ground black pepper*
> *3 sprigs rosemary*
> *4 cloves garlic*
> *1 small tunnel-boned leg of lamb*
> *2 ounces quince paste, melted*

Mix a slug of olive oil and the lemon juice, salt, pepper, and rosemary in a bowl. Cut the garlic into slivers. Pierce the meat several times with a sharp knife, then push the garlic slivers into these holes. Put the meat in a baking dish and pour the olive-oil mixture over it. Marinate the meat for 1 hour, turning it several times.

Prepare a wood fire. Heat the grill and cook the lamb at least 2½ inches above the fire, turning it regularly and brushing it each time with the melted quince paste. The cooking time will depend on the size of the leg, but allow about 30 minutes, then cover and allow it to rest before carving. The meat will retain its heat, so don't be tempted to rest it for anything less than 15 minutes, preferably longer.

SERVES 6

CARROTS, ONIONS, POTATOES, AND FENNEL ROASTED TOGETHER

STEPHANIE ✒ This dish shows some similarity to the second variation included with the recipe for stewed artichokes on page 72. The process of cooking vegetables without much liquid is a useful one to understand.

We also considered adding the cardoons and baby artichokes we saw in markets. Cardoons are in fact related to artichokes and resemble a huge thistle, but it is the leaf stalk that is eaten rather than the flower. The prepared stems are often stewed in olive oil with onion and garlic or chopped to add to a vegetable stew, soup, or creamy gratin or, as happened at lunch with Ann and Aldo (see page 76), diced to make fritters. Maggie made careful note of how cardoons were grown in Tuscany since she has this vegetable in her garden, but has not had much success with it. The Tuscans removed the old and discolored leaves and drew the stems together, then wrapped them with paper before banking soil around them for six weeks as is done with celery.

Parsnips would be another good inclusion, although we didn't see them in Italy.

ABOVE Roasted chunks of vegetables in one of Anna Rosa's lovely baking dishes. A drizzle of vinegar in the last fifteen minutes of cooking produces wonderful caramelization.

carrots, peeled and cut into bite-sized chunks

small onions, peeled

small potatoes, peeled or unpeeled

fennel bulbs, quartered

olive oil

sea salt

freshly ground black pepper

unpeeled garlic cloves

lemons (optional)

balsamic or good aged red-wine vinegar

Preheat the oven to 400°F. Toss the vegetables in a large bowl with plenty of olive oil, salt, and pepper, then add a good number of fat, firm garlic cloves. (A few halved lemons are also good additions, not for eating but for the flavor the peel gives the vegetables.) Roast in a heavy-based baking pan in the oven, stirring and shaking to prevent the vegetables from sticking. The vegetables need at least 1½ hours.

For the last 15 minutes of cooking, drizzle the vegetables with balsamic or red-wine vinegar. Transfer the pan to the grill or stove for this last stage to allow the vinegar to caramelize and give wonderful sticky brown edges to the vegetable chunks.

CARAMEL CHOCOLATE PUDDINGS

We served these glazed, beautiful puddings with Antinori *vin santo*, which picked up the marzipan flavors in the *amaretti*.

ABOVE We served caramel chocolate puddings one night with a purée of plums instead of the *Amaro*-flavored sauce given here. The hint of bitter almonds in the *amaretti* cookies makes the puddings a very satisfying and sophisticated dessert. The same slightly bitter, herby character is present in the *Amaro*. This delicious fortified Italian *digestivo* deserves to be better known.

butter, softened
1½ cups crumbled amaretti cookies
1 cup milk
¼ cup cream
scant ½ cup sugar
3 eggs, separated
⅓ cup Dutch cocoa
CARAMEL
¼ cup water
1 cup sugar
APPLE AND AMARO SAUCE
6 eating apples
2 tablespoons water
½ cup sugar
scented leaves (lemon verbena, geranium, myrtle, bay) or 1 vanilla bean
¼ cup Amaro, grappa, or brandy

Preheat the oven to 350°F. To make the caramel, stir the water and sugar in a saucepan over heat until the sugar has dissolved. Stop stirring and cook until a deep-caramel color. Remove the caramel from the heat and immediately dip the base of the pan into cold water to stop the cooking. Pour the caramel into eight 4-ounce (125 ml) pudding molds, tilting to spread the caramel. Butter any exposed surfaces.

Soak the crumbled cookies in the milk and cream. Cream 3 tablespoons butter and the sugar in a food processor, then add the egg yolks one at a time. Add the cocoa and cookies but do not overprocess. Whisk the egg whites until snowy peaks form, then fold this gently into the cookie mixture. Fill the molds with the mixture, then stand them in a baking tray lined with a dish towel and pour in hot water to come two-thirds of the way up their sides. Cover the whole tray with foil and bake for 25–30 minutes until the puddings feel springy but not solid when pressed lightly. Remove the puddings from the oven but leave the foil in place for 5 minutes to minimize falling. Cool, if desired.

While the puddings are cooking, make the apple and *Amaro* sauce. Peel, core, and slice the apples finely. Put the apple into a saucepan with the water, sugar, and leaves or vanilla bean. Simmer gently until quite soft. Remove the leaves or vanilla bean and press the apple and its liquid through a sieve or blend quickly in a food processor. Stir in the *Amaro* to taste. Serve the warm sauce with warm or cold puddings.

SERVES 8

ANFORTE

STEPHANIE ❧ Siena is the home of *panforte* and as one would expect every boutique that sold *prodotti tipici* had a large selection. We became very discriminating, preferring the darker, spicier versions. Those I have bought in Siena were moister than the versions I have made myself, but all keep extremely well. I have had a *panforte* in my own pantry cupboard for well over a year and from time to time remember to cut myself a small slice.

I do not claim the following cake to be the same as we ate in Siena. After my recent experience, I would replace some of the apricots with candied orange and citron peel.

ABOVE Traditionally wrapped *panforte* bought in Siena.

> 6 ounces dark couverture chocolate
>
> 4 cups almonds, lightly toasted
>
> 1½ cups honey
>
> 1 cup sugar
>
> 1 cup glacé figs, chopped
>
> 1¼ cups glacé apricots, chopped
>
> ½ cup glacé ginger, chopped
>
> 2¼ cups all-purpose flour
>
> ¾ cup best-quality Dutch cocoa
>
> 1 tablespoon cinnamon
>
> 2 teaspoons ground white pepper
>
> 2 teaspoons ground allspice

Bring a saucepan of water to a full boil, then turn the heat down very low. Put the chocolate into a bowl wide enough to be suspended by the saucepan and place it over the hot water. Cover tightly with a lid, plastic wrap, or foil, so that neither water nor steam will spoil the chocolate (a drop of moisture will cause the chocolate to seize). Allow the chocolate to melt slowly, then set aside to cool.

Preheat the oven to 300°F. Stir the honey and sugar in a saucepan over a moderate heat until the sugar has dissolved. Remove any stray sugar crystals on the side of the pan with a pastry brush dipped in cold water. Place a warmed candy thermometer in the pan and bring the syrup to a boil. Have another pan of cold water and a small bowl of cold water with ice cubes in it at the ready. Cook the syrup until the thermometer registers 230°F. Dip the pan in the cold water and immediately drop a teaspoonful of syrup into the iced water and test if it makes a soft ball between your fingers. If it drops away immediately, return the pan to the heat and boil until the thermometer reads 240°F, then test the syrup again. When the syrup is ready, stir in the chocolate, then pour this over the remaining ingredients in a bowl and mix very well. Pour the mixture into an 11-inch springform pan or a 1½-inch deep baking tray and bake for 30 minutes. Allow to cool completely in the pan before cutting.

A ntique platters piled with purple grapes, vases filled with scented lilies and glossy bay leaves evoking Caravaggio, game birds in various guises, special puddings of *porcini*,

exquisitely presented desserts and wines: these splendid evenings celebrated the best of Tuscany and were deliberately theatrical.

The Banquet

ANZAROTTI

STEPHANIE ✿ Each of our cooking school sessions ended with a banquet to celebrate all that had been learned during the week and to bid farewell to the students. For each one Tony created a theme for the dining room. For the first banquet the room was reminiscent of some sumptuous film set: richly purple grapes were arranged on antique platters and vases were filled with scented lilies and glossy bay leaves evoking Caravaggio. Silver candlesticks were polished, and the table was set with Anna Rosa's best embroidered cloth. Riotous displays of sunflower-yellow daisies in huge quantities and creamy lilies and tuberoses set the mood for the second banquet. But it was for the third banquet that Tony outdid himself. The flowers were red, white, and green, and a still life included a cock and hen pheasant in full feather.

MAGGIE ✿ We began each banquet with Antinori Spumante Brut and either Elena's *pizzette* or the following *panzarotti*. For the second banquet, I used semihard goat cheese, buffalo *mozzarella*, and aged *pecorino* in the filling, and substituted local *salami* for the ham in the original recipe. The result was better than I could have expected: as we bit into the golden, light-as-a-feather pastries, the cheese oozed out and the flavors of the *salami* came through.

This recipe is based on one in Claudia Roden's *The Food of Italy*. It's best to prepare the stuffing and the dough the day before. This allows the flavors in the stuffing to meld thoroughly—just remember to allow extra time to drain the *ricotta* overnight in a muslin-lined sieve. The pastry is made with a good amount of olive oil so it won't deteriorate if refrigerated well covered. While the instructions given here involve filling the *panzarotti* at the last minute, the pastry can in fact be rolled and filled in the morning, and the pastries refrigerated until required for cooking that night.

olive oil for deep-frying

DOUGH

4 cups all-purpose flour

5 eggs

⅓ cup olive oil

salt

FILLING

9 ounces ricotta, drained overnight

2 eggs

3½ ounces pecorino, finely chopped

8 ounces buffalo mozzarella, finely diced

8 ounces salami, finely diced

⅓ cup freshly grated Parmigiano-Reggiano

1 cup freshly chopped Italian (flat-leaved) parsley

salt

freshly ground black pepper

Make the dough (it's like pasta dough) the day before you plan to serve the *panzarotti*. Put the flour into a bowl, then make a well in the center and break in the eggs. Add the olive oil and a little salt. Mix it all with a fork at first and then with your fingers. Knead well for 6–8 minutes to form a smooth, silky, elastic dough, dusting it with flour if it becomes sticky. Wrap the dough in plastic wrap and refrigerate overnight (if making the *panzarotti* the day you wish to serve them, rest the dough for at least 30 minutes). Meanwhile, mix all the filling ingredients in a large bowl and refrigerate overnight.

About an hour before serving, roll out the dough as thinly as possible, then cut it into rectangles about 4 x 12 inches. Place little spoonfuls of the filling along one long side about ½ inch from the edge, leaving 1 inch between each mound. Wet the edge slightly and fold the dough over, pressing to ensure the edges stick together. Using a glass or a round pastry cutter, cut along the folded seam to make half-moon shapes. Decorate the cut edge using a fork or fold the edge over. Let the half-moons rest for 30 minutes (the *panzarotti* can also be prepared to this stage in the morning if serving them that night).

Meanwhile, heat a good quantity of olive oil in a deep saucepan until very hot. Lower a few *panzarotti* into the oil at a time, then turn down the heat slightly so that they do not burn. Cook for a very short time, turning once; they will brown and crisp quickly. Remove the *panzarotti* and drain on crumpled paper towels. Allow to cool a little after cooking as the filling will be very hot.

MAKES ABOUT 40

FETTUCCINE WITH TRUFFLES

MAGGIE 🐚 The truffle supply at the Florence market was a bit erratic, and some we bought proved to be no good once we cut into them back at the villa. We returned to the stall to follow up on the promise of fresh truffles and were delighted to be offered a huge 7-ounce specimen, but were aghast at the price! Although we could see it hurt him to do so, the very handsome and charming stallholder offered to cut the truffle in half for us. We'd realized from our earlier mistake that it's better to buy half a large truffle than smaller ones since the texture can be examined before purchase, although it's a kind truffle-seller who will agree to this. (A truffle can bear evidence of past visitations from worms, which leave it crumbly—a very nasty surprise.) There was much banter, all in great humor, and we ended up with 3½ ounces at a reduced rate. Honor was satisfied on all sides!

If you are not cooking the pasta immediately, it is important to allow time for it to dry. See the instructions for this on page 212. If you want to cook for more people, allow ⅓ ounce of truffle per person.

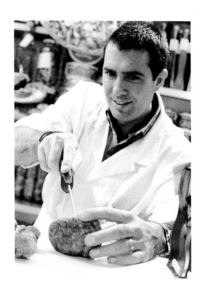

ABOVE The handsome and charming stallholder at the San Lorenzo market bravely halving a huge truffle for us.

OPPOSITE On the night of the banquet for the second cooking school session there was a collective gasp as Maggie removed the lid of the jar in which our truffles were stored. The aroma instantly filled the very large dining room. She shaved the truffles all over the freshly made and cooked *fettuccine* for a stunning beginning to the meal. We all decided on the spot that we needed to buy a truffle cutter, so fine and delicate were the resulting wafers.

1 quantity Maggie's Fresh Egg Pasta (see page 211)
salt
¾ cup unsalted butter
½ cup white wine
freshly ground black pepper
pinch of nutmeg
⅓ cup freshly grated Parmigiano-Reggiano
3½ ounces white truffle

Bring a large pot of water to a boil. Make the pasta as instructed, then using a pasta machine put one of the pieces of dough through the maximum aperture 8–10 times until shiny and silky. Pass the dough 3–4 times through the remaining settings until you reach the second-to-last setting. Run the pasta sheets through the *fettuccine* cutters. Add salt to the boiling water and cook the pasta until *al dente*—this will only take a couple of minutes—noting that additional cooking will occur when the sauce is added to the pasta.

While the pasta is cooking, melt the butter in a large saucepan, then add the wine and cook briskly over a high heat to reduce it a little. Season with salt and pepper and a pinch of nutmeg. Drain the pasta and toss with the melted butter mixture. Remove the pan from the heat, then mix in the *Parmigiano-Reggiano*. Transfer to a warm platter, then shave the white truffle over the pasta and serve immediately on hot plates.

SERVES 10–12

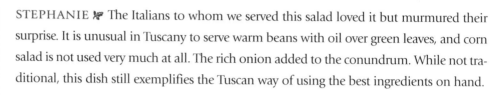Bean Salad with Caramelized Onions and Artichokes

STEPHANIE 🐝 The Italians to whom we served this salad loved it but murmured their surprise. It is unusual in Tuscany to serve warm beans with oil over green leaves, and corn salad is not used very much at all. The rich onion added to the conundrum. While not traditional, this dish still exemplifies the Tuscan way of using the best ingredients on hand.

ABOVE We could not buy truffles for two of our banquets, so instead served this very delicious salad on rosettes of tender corn salad (also known as lamb's lettuce, *mache*, or, in Italian, *valeriana*). The salad draws on three components that were featured in various ways on our menus: beans, caramelized onions, and artichokes stewed in olive oil. In a bid not to waste anything, we used the cooking liquid from the beans to make *minestrone* (see page 156) and the sauce for the *sformato* on page 196.

OPPOSITE Detail from work in Museo Civico, San Gimignano.

7 ounces freshly shelled cannellini beans or 3½ ounces dried beans, soaked overnight

1 onion, finely chopped

1 stick celery, finely chopped

1 fresh bay leaf

1 sprig thyme

3 cloves garlic

stewed artichokes (see page 72)

freshly ground black pepper

salt

corn salad or arugula

freshly chopped Italian (flat-leaved) parsley

CARAMELIZED ONIONS

20 small or pickling onions, peeled

½ cup extra-virgin olive oil

1 bay leaf

1 sprig rosemary

To make the caramelized onions, quarter or slice the onions, then put all the ingredients into a heavy-based or nonstick frying pan. Cook, covered, over a moderate heat for 15 minutes until the onion has begun to soften, stirring frequently. Remove the cover and cook, stirring, until the onion has separated and is turning a rich caramel. Don't worry if sections look very dark—this adds flavor—just stir frequently to prevent sticking. (If this looks likely, add oil.) The onions keep well in their oil in the refrigerator for several days.

Put the beans into a large saucepan and cover with water. Add the onion, celery, herbs, and garlic and simmer, covered, for 45 minutes or until tender (if using dried beans, use more water and cook for 1½ hours). Pour the beans into a bowl and allow to cool in their liquid. Drain the cooled beans, reserving the liquid but discarding the herbs. Heat some of the oil from the caramelized onions in a wide-based saucepan and add the drained beans and 1 cup cooking liquid. Simmer over a moderate heat until creamy, then season. Toss the beans with plenty of caramelized onions and stewed artichokes. Spoon the salad onto a bed of corn salad and sprinkle with parsley.

SERVES 6

SFORMATO OF PORCINI WITH BONE MARROW AND PORCINI SAUCE

STEPHANIE ❧ I began the *sformato* sauce three days before the second banquet, and made the puddings the day before. This is another example of impromptu cooking coming about because we couldn't bear to waste anything, in this case the soaking liquid from the *porcini* and the cooking liquid from the beans used in the salad that preceded this dish (see page 194). I used the bean cooking liquid in place of the *brodo* listed below. The flavors of the finished dish were superb and complex. The sauce was bound with just a whisper of cream, and we slipped a slice of poached bone marrow onto each plate.

We had no problem buying shin bones full of marrow at San Lorenzo market. The butcher deftly cut each bone so that we had convenient 2½-inch sections. Back at the villa we pushed the marrow from the bones and then soaked it in lightly salted water until it was needed (the marrow can stay like this, refrigerated, for two days).

butter

½ cup all-purpose flour

1½ cups warm milk

2½ ounces ricotta

1 tablespoon freshly grated Parmigiano-Reggiano

2 tablespoons freshly chopped Italian (flat-leaved) parsley

1 cup sliced porcini or field mushrooms

1 tablespoon dry marsala

3 egg yolks

salt

freshly ground black pepper

4 egg whites

2 cups cream

SAUCE

1 handful dried porcini

1¾ cups warm water

¼ cup butter

3 cups freshly sliced porcini, field or pine mushrooms

1 teaspoon chopped garlic

1½ cups Nebbiolo or other dry red wine

1¾ cups Chicken Brodo (see page 213) or reserved bean soaking liquid

salt

pepper

½ cup cream

¼ cup bone marrow

To make the sauce, reconstitute the dried *porcini* in the warm water for 20 minutes, then remove and squeeze any moisture back into the soaking liquid. Finely chop the *porcini* (you should have about 1 cup) and set aside. Strain the soaking liquid through a doubled layer of muslin and reserve (you should have about ¾ cup).

Heat the butter in a wide-based frying pan until foaming, then add the fresh mushrooms and cook for 5 minutes. Add the garlic and the reconstituted *porcini* and cook over a brisk heat for another 5 minutes. Stir in 1 cup of the red wine, then increase the heat and reduce the contents to a moist mixture. Add the remaining wine, the reserved strained *porcini* liquid and the *brodo* and simmer for 10 minutes. Taste for salt and pepper.

Preheat the oven to 350°F. Melt a knob of butter and grease twelve 4-ounce (125 ml) soufflé dishes. Melt ¼ cup butter in a small heavy-based saucepan. Add the flour and cook over a moderate heat, stirring, for 2 minutes. Gradually add the warm milk, stirring all the while (you can substitute bean soaking liquid left over from another dish for a third of the milk, if you like). Bring to a boil, then reduce the heat and simmer for 5 minutes, then remove from the heat. Break up the *ricotta* with a fork until it is soft and add it to this mixture with the *Parmigiano-Reggiano* and the parsley. Allow to cool for a few minutes.

Meanwhile, sauté the mushrooms in a little butter until softened, then stir in the marsala. Fold the egg yolks into the *ricotta* mixture thoroughly. Taste the mixture for salt and pepper and fold in the mushrooms. Beat the egg whites until creamy and quickly fold into the *ricotta* and mushroom mixture.

Divide the mixture among the prepared molds and smooth the surface of each. Place the molds in a baking dish lined with a dish towel and pour in boiling water to come two-thirds up their sides. Bake for about 20 minutes until firm to the touch and well puffed. Remove from the oven—the "puddings" will deflate and look wrinkled. Allow to rest for a minute, then ease each pudding out of its mold.

Just before serving, preheat the oven to 400°F. To finish off the sauce, heat the ½ cup cream until boiling with big, fat bubbles. Reheat the mushroom sauce in another pan, then stir this into the hot cream. Poach the sliced bone marrow in water for 3 minutes, then remove from the pan and keep warm.

Place the puddings, well spaced, in a buttered baking dish, then spoon 2 tablespoons of cream over each one. Bake for 15 minutes until swollen and pale golden on top. Carefully lift each pudding onto a hot plate, then spoon the sauce around and slip some bone marrow in among the mushrooms and serve.

SERVES 12

ABOVE These superb twice-baked savory "puddings" are clay-colored, just like the *Crete di Siena*, the primeval landscape south of Siena. Isole e Olena vintner Paolo de Marchi, a guest at our second banquet with his wife, Marta, had spoken during the cooking school of the importance of a grapegrower and winemaker "reading the landscape," and here we had achieved it with food!

Pheasant in Vin Santo with Chestnuts and Pancetta

Before we set out for Italy, we decided that the main dish for each banquet would be pheasant—only to find that sourcing pheasant in Italy wasn't as easy as we'd anticipated (and what we did find tended to be riddled with shot). There was so much change between what we predicted we'd cook for these celebratory dinners and what we ended up doing—a reflection on the ripeness and seasonal nature of Italian produce and of our philosophy to "go with the flow." While we cooked guinea fowl for the banquets at Villa di Corsano, we include our original recipe here for the simple reason that it is delicious.

2 cups Chicken Brodo (see page 213)
2 pheasants, each 2¼ pounds
vin santo
1½ tablespoons butter
olive oil
7 ounces peeled fresh or frozen chestnuts
7 ounces tiny onions, peeled
salt
freshly ground black pepper
12 slices pancetta
MARINADE
½ cup olive oil
juice of 1 orange
4 strips orange zest
4 sprigs thyme
2 bay leaves
1 teaspoon crushed juniper berries

OPPOSITE Our in-house art director Tony outdid himself at our final banquet. The focus was a still life of a cock and hen pheasant in full feather in one of the windows to the dining room.

Reduce the *brodo* over heat until 1 cup remains. Cut away the backbone from each pheasant, then flatten the frame with the heel of your hand to splay each bird out. Remove any blood from inside the birds. Combine the ingredients for the marinade in a bowl. Brush the entire skin of the pheasants with the marinade, adding more olive oil if necessary to ensure the marinade adheres. Marinate the pheasants for two hours. Reserve any extra marinade.

➥ *page 200*

Preheat the oven to 475°F. Roast the pheasants for 10 minutes, skin-side up, to caramelize. Turn the birds over to seal the other side and finish the cooking, about another 10 minutes. Check to see if the birds are cooked by pulling a leg away from the breast. It should come away easily. While still pink, the meat should show no sign of rawness. Remove the cooked birds and rest them, skin-side down, covered with foil on a warm plate. Don't turn off the oven—you'll need it again soon.

Place the baking dish over a high heat on the stove and deglaze with ½ cup *vin santo* and any remaining marinade, stirring well to catch any caramelized bits. Add the *brodo* to the pan and reduce to make a sauce.

Heat the butter in a heavy-based frying pan until nut-brown, then add a touch of olive oil. Add the chestnuts and onions and cook until partly softened, then add a splash of *vin santo* and cover the pan to finish the cooking.

Add the onions and chestnuts to the sauce and reduce to the desired consistency. Check the seasoning. Crisp the *pancetta* for a couple of minutes on a cookie sheet in the hot oven and add it to the resting pheasants. Present the roasted pheasants and *pancetta* on a serving platter with the sauce to one side.

SERVES 4

BELOW AND OPPOSITE Plucking the pheasants. These were wild birds, and we found them rich and gamey— and complete with the odd bit of buckshot.

GUINEA FOWL WITH CITRUS

OPPOSITE Guinea Fowl with Citrus: game, orange, and juniper berries are a special marriage. By the morning of the last banquet the party was winding down, and we had run out of juniper berries. The day was saved when our forest walk yielded fresh berries. We picked a thorny juniper branch or two and pocketed them until back in the kitchen.

MAGGIE ❧ This dish took different forms for each banquet, depending on what treasures were available in the market. The guinea fowl was particularly good with the juicy *miagawa*, a Sicilian orange that was deep, deep green on the outside, brilliant orange inside, and midway between a lemon and an orange in flavor. For one banquet I used clementines, a variety of tangerine and like a sweet orange. For another I stuffed truffle paste made with breadcrumbs and butter under the skin and rubbed the birds with truffle oil. If guinea fowl are unavailable, Cornish game hens are an acceptable substitute.

3 guinea fowl, each 1¾ pounds

3 oranges, bitter oranges, mandarins, limes, or 12 kumquats

6 fresh bay leaves

6 fine slices pancetta

6 small flat onions or 12 shallots

extra-virgin olive oil

3 large braised heads of Belgian endive or 2 small braised fennel bulbs (see page 205)

MARINADE

juice of 2 oranges

8 strips orange zest

8 sprigs thyme

4 fresh bay leaves

2 teaspoons crushed juniper berries

olive oil

SAUCE

1 large onion, roughly chopped

2 small carrots, roughly chopped

2 sticks celery, roughly chopped

extra-virgin olive oil

½ cup vin santo

2¼ cups Chicken Brodo (see page 213)

Preheat the oven to 475°F. Cut away the backbone from each guinea fowl, then flatten the frame with the heel of your hand to splay each bird out. Remove any blood from inside the birds. Combine the marinade ingredients in a bowl, adding just enough olive oil to moisten the mixture. Brush the entire skin of the guinea fowl with the marinade, adding more olive oil if necessary to ensure the marinade adheres. Marinate the guinea fowl for 2 hours. Reserve any remaining marinade, setting a separate few tablespoons aside for the guinea fowl salad on page 204.

Slice the oranges thickly and divide them between two baking dishes with the bay leaves, *pancetta*, and onions and drizzle with olive oil. Add the guinea fowl and roast for

10 minutes, skin-side up, to caramelize. Turn the birds over to seal the other side and finish the cooking, about another 10 minutes. (The onions should also be caramelized by this time.) Check to see if the birds are cooked by pulling a leg away from the breast. It should come away easily. While still pink, the meat should show no sign of rawness. Remove the cooked birds and rest them, skin-side down, covered with foil on a warm plate for 20 minutes minimum. Transfer the orange, onions, and *pancetta* to one of the baking dishes. Don't turn off the oven—you'll need it again soon.

To carve each guinea fowl, separate the leg from the breast, then the thigh from the leg. Remove the thigh bones and set the thigh meat aside, with its skin intact and the cut side returned to the juices that have accumulated, for the dish below. Carve the breast from the frame and add to the dish with the drumsticks, orange, onions, and *pancetta*. Chop the carcasses and set aside.

To make the sauce, roast the onion, carrot, and celery with a drizzle of olive oil for 20 minutes until caramelized. Deglaze the baking dish with the vegetables in it over high heat by adding the *vin santo* and any remaining marinade, stirring well. Add the carcasses and pour in the *brodo*, then boil rapidly to reduce the sauce (it shouldn't be too thick). Strain the sauce and discard the solids. Cut each braised Belgian endive head in half (if using fennel, cut each braised bulb in three), then add to the dish with the oranges and so on.

Remove the leg meat from the baking dish. Arrange the breast meat evenly in the baking dish with the onions, orange, *pancetta*, and Belgian endive or fennel and heat in the oven for 2–3 minutes. Set the *pancetta* aside for use in the salad below. Bring the sauce to a rolling boil. Add the leg meat to the breast meat and so on, then moisten everything with the hot sauce, and divide among hot plates to serve.

SERVES 6

GUINEA FOWL SALAD WITH WALNUTS, LIVER, & RADICCHIO

We served this salad to follow whichever version of the guinea fowl dish we cooked (see page 202). Dry-roast 6 freshly shelled walnuts for 6–8 minutes at 400°F, then rub off their skins with a clean dish towel, if not freshly picked. Brush the reserved guinea fowl thigh meat with the reserved marinade and grill quickly on a hot broiler pan or grill, turning the meat at right angles to achieve a criss-cross pattern on the skin, then set aside. Sauté 6 guinea fowl or chicken livers in a heavy-based frying pan until sealed and firm but still pink inside. Choose 6 tightly curled, inner *radicchio* leaves, then fill these with the meat, liver, and walnuts and add the *pancetta* cooked in the above recipe. Serve immediately dressed with a vinaigrette of mellow extra-virgin olive oil, a little freshly squeezed lemon and orange juice, salt, and freshly ground black pepper.

BRAISED ENDIVE OR FENNEL

Braising relies on a relatively small amount of liquid compared with the main ingredient. The liquid surrounds and nourishes the main ingredient and each gives its flavors to the other. If the cooking time is judged properly, the liquid will have become a sauce just as the main ingredient is ready. Choosing an appropriately sized dish is very important.

Because of its attractive bitterness this dish is good served with something that is quite bland in flavor, such as a roasted quail, or alternatively with something rather rich that can do with having its richness offset by bitterness, such as a hamhock, squab, pheasant, game hen, or guinea fowl.

Fennel is equally good prepared this way—just choose small bulbs.

butter
Belgian endive heads or fennel bulbs
salt
freshly ground black pepper
Brodo (see page 213)

ABOVE Tony arranging flowers for a banquet night.

Preheat the oven to 350°F. Butter a gratin dish in which the required number of Belgian endive heads or halved fennel bulbs will just fit. Roll the vegetables in melted butter, then arrange in the dish and season. Pour the *brodo* over the vegetables to come halfway up their sides. Press a piece of baking parchment cut to fit right down over the vegetables and cover with a lid or a doubled piece of foil. Bake for 20 minutes.

Remove the dish from the oven and turn the vegetables. Return the dish to the oven, uncovered and without the baking parchment, for an additional 20 minutes. The vegetables should be tender and the sauce reduced and sticky. If the vegetables are cooked but still swimming in juice, remove them to a warm plate and boil the liquid hard on the stove. Return the vegetables to the dish when only a few spoonfuls of liquid are left, just enough to give a shiny and sticky finish.

SAUSAGES OR MEATBALLS
By adding small, well-flavored sausages or meatballs to the braising pan, one creates an entire meal with very little effort. This is a lovely way to cook: one knows that all the flavors will combine deliciously and a little more cooking time will never matter if it seems that the juices need more reducing or the sausages need additional browning.

⌑ L DUOMO (ZUCCOTTO)

For our final banquet twenty-two gathered around the table, with Tony, Elena, and Peter all sitting down whenever they could to share in the fun. Anna Rosa and Constantino, her husband, were our guests. They were charmed by Tony's red, white, and green flower arrangements.

The *zuccotto* was made and presented by Elena with help from Tony, who had decorated it with rows of silver balls and diamonds of our beautiful candied ruby grapefruit with the same care and attention he would give to a costume for *Hello Dolly*. And Elena had secretly prepared some "M" and "S" chocolate letters (for Maggie and Stephanie, of course), a pair for each portion. The *zuccotto* had a *cupola* on top made from peaches, and the *grappa* syrup was tinted pink with the juice of blood oranges. The effect was of a dome bathed in the colors of a rosy sunset.

THESE PAGES Elena presenting the *zuccotto*. Marcella Hazan says in *The Classic Italian Cookbook* that this Florentine specialty is inspired by the dome of that city's cathedral. The dessert is formed by lining a large bowl with cake—the crusts represent the ribbing of Brunelleschi's famous dome.

CAKE

1½ cups all-purpose flour

1½ teaspoons baking powder

pinch of salt

1 tablespoon lemon juice

¼ cup milk

½ cup unsalted butter, softened

¾ cup sugar

3 eggs

LEMON SYRUP

¼ cup water

¾ cup sugar

¼ cup lemon juice

¼ cup orange juice

¼ cup limoncello or grappa

FILLING

7 ounces bittersweet couverture chocolate

1 cup cream

1 scant cup powdered sugar

1 cup mascarpone

3½ ounces drained ricotta

1 cup blanched almonds, roughly chopped

1 cup toasted hazelnuts, skins rubbed off and roughly chopped

½ cup candied citron, grapefruit, or lemon peel (see page 69), chopped

Preheat the oven to 325°F. To make the cake, grease a 9 x 5 x 3 inch loaf pan and line it with baking parchment. Sift the flour, baking powder, and salt together. Mix the lemon juice into the milk and set aside. Cream the butter and sugar until thick and pale, then add the eggs one at a time, beating thoroughly after each. Lightly beat in one-third of the flour. Add half the milk and lemon juice and the remaining flour and combine very lightly. Spoon the mixture into the prepared pan and bake for about 1 hour or until a skewer inserted into the center comes out clean. Turn the cake out from the pan onto a wire rack and allow to cool completely before cutting.

Meanwhile, put a mixing bowl into the refrigerator to chill it. To make the syrup, gently heat the water and sugar in a saucepan, stirring until the sugar has dissolved. Add the lemon and orange juice. Remove the pan from the heat and stir in your chosen liqueur.

Cut the cake into ¼-inch slices, then cut each slice in half on the diagonal. Paint the cake slices lightly with the lemon syrup, then line a 1½-quart round-bottomed bowl with the cake, the point of each slice toward the bottom and a crust meeting a noncrust edge to echo the lines of the famous dome (keep the ribs of the dome in mind as you do this and you won't go wrong—when the dessert is inverted, the "ribs" run down the cake). Ensure that the surface of the bowl is completely covered. Patch any holes with more moistened cake. You should have enough cake left to make the lid later on. Reserve any leftover syrup.

To make the filling, chop or grate half the chocolate. Carefully melt the remaining chocolate in a bowl standing over a saucepan of simmering hot water. Remove the pan from the heat and allow the chocolate to cool but not set.

Whip the cream and powdered sugar in the chilled mixing bowl until very stiff. Blend the *mascarpone* in a food processor to soften it, then whisk it with the *ricotta*. Fold this mixture into the sweetened whipped cream. Mix in the nuts, candied peel, and chopped or grated chocolate. Put a third of the mixture into a bowl, then add the cooled melted chocolate and fold through thoroughly.

Spread the mixture without the melted chocolate over the moistened cake in the bowl, smoothing it evenly and leaving a hole in the center. Fill the center of the bowl with the chocolate mixture and level off the top. Cover the top with the reserved slices of moistened cake. Cover the bowl with plastic wrap and refrigerate overnight or for 24 hours.

To unmold, carefully invert the *zuccotto* onto a plate and moisten the cake with the reserved syrup if it looks at all dry. Serve cut into wedges with a compote of poached fruits alongside or just as it is.

SERVES 10

The
Pantry
Garlic Oil

Throughout the cooking schools we kept a good quantity of very finely chopped garlic thoroughly mixed with extra-virgin olive oil in a jar. The oil covered the garlic by a half inch and kept beautifully, refrigerated, for at least a week. We brushed it on grilling meat and vegetables and used whenever an extra flavor boost was needed.

Mushrooms

PRESERVING MUSHROOMS

This is based on one in Antonio Carluccio's *An Invitation to Italian Cooking*, although the sterilization procedure, where the filled and sealed jars are heated, is our addition. Many traditional recipes omit any mention of this step. While we both have great confidence in traditional methods, we prefer to err on the side of caution when teaching about preserving.

In Italy the magnificent, meaty *porcini* would be preserved in this manner, but firm, cultivated mushrooms can be substituted very successfully. Either kind makes a wonderful addition to an *antipasto* platter.

> *2¼ pounds mushrooms*
> *3 cups white-wine vinegar*
> *1¼ cups verjuice (see page 219)*
> *3 fresh bay leaves*
> *3 cloves garlic*
> *1 tablespoon salt*
> *olive oil*

Clean the mushrooms, discarding any that are not firm. Bring the vinegar and verjuice to a boil in a large enameled or stainless steel saucepan, then add the bay leaves, garlic, salt, and mushrooms. Cook for 6 minutes, keeping the mushrooms immersed in the boiling liquid. Remove the mushrooms with a slotted spoon to a clean, dry dish towel, stem-side down. Strain the cooking liquid, then reserve it and the bay leaves and garlic.

Pour a little olive oil into a sterilized preserving jar, then add a layer of mushrooms, a clove of garlic, and a bay leaf, then cover with more oil and press the mushrooms down with a spoon to remove any air bubbles. Continue layering the mushrooms, then cover well with olive oil.

Seal the filled jars, then wrap each in a sheet of paper and use a rubber band to hold it in place. Place the jars in a large stockpot. Fill the pot with cold water to the level of the lids, then bring it to a boil and maintain a full boil for 1½ hours. Allow the jars to cool in the water. Unwrap and dry the jars and store away from the light.

MAKES 1.5 QUARTS

IN OIL

Slice the mushrooms thickly, then sprinkle them with salt and leave for 1 hour. Wipe dry. Heat a thin layer of olive oil in a frying pan and quickly sauté the mushrooms to remove some of their liquid. Pack the mushrooms into sterilized preserving jars, then add a few peppercorns and cover with olive oil. Proceed as above.

IN THEIR OWN JUICES

Wipe the mushrooms clean. Keep the mushrooms whole unless they are very large (in this case, halve or quarter them). Add the juice of 2–3 lemons to a large saucepan of salted water and bring to a boil. Drop in the mushrooms and boil for 3 minutes. Drain the mushrooms and pack them tightly into sterilized preserving jars interspersed with extra salt and a few peppercorns. Proceed as above.

ANGELO BONACCI'S METHOD

Angelo and Mary Bonacci live in Myrtleford, Victoria in Australia, and their cellar displays row upon row of preserved fruit and vegetables—jars of cherries, figs, peaches, peppers, corn, pickled eggplant, and preserved mushrooms. Angelo's method is described here. Clean the mushrooms and cut them into small pieces. Bring equal quantities of vinegar and water and plenty of salt (to discourage mold) to a boil in a saucepan and cook the mushrooms for 15 minutes. Drain the mushrooms, then dry them on a clean dish towel and leave overnight. Next day, put the mushrooms into an enamel or stainless steel container, interspersed with chopped garlic, parsley, and dried oregano. Cover with olive oil and soak overnight. Pack into sterilized jars; cover completely with olive oil.

Pasta

MAGGIE'S FRESH EGG PASTA

Fresh pasta made by hand is quite different from that made in a food processor. The kneading—anything from 10–20 minutes, depending on your skill—results in a wonderfully shiny dough.

While pasta dough can be rolled out and then cut into strips, the inexpensive, easy-to-use Italian pasta machines available from good kitchen suppliers makes this job easy. These hand-operated "machines" screw onto a benchtop and consist of three pairs of rollers, two of which knead and then roll out the dough; the third set cuts the final pasta sheet. The rollers are governed by a knob on the side of the machine that allows you to change the width of the gap between the rollers. When the pasta dough is first fed through the machine, the rollers are set on the widest aperture, then you work your way through the settings until you are ready to cut the pasta sheet, which by now is long and fine from rolling. The machines usually come with a couple of different cutters, perhaps *spaghetti* and *fettuccine*. Other cutters can be bought separately.

When feeding the dough through the widest setting, you are essentially kneading it. To get the best results, fold the ends of the dough in over the center of the sheet until you have a "parcel" a third the size of the original sheet. Run this through the machine once more, then fold and roll and so on. When you move on to the next setting you don't need to fold the dough, but it is advisable to run it through the machine several times. The more the pasta is put through the rollers, the finer the result. You may find it useful to ask someone to "catch" the pasta sheet as it comes off the rollers, while you continue to feed in the dough. It may also be necessary to cut the sheet into a manageable length—the longer you feed it through the rollers, the longer the sheet! Feeding the pasta sheet through the second-to-last setting several times at the end will help achieve perfect pasta. Once the pasta sheet is as fine as you require, feed it through the cutters.

This quantity of pasta yields 6–12 servings.

4¼ cups unbleached all-purpose flour
salt
4 large eggs
6 egg yolks
4 quarts water

Pour the flour mixed with 1 teaspoon salt onto a work surface and make a well in the center. Whisk the eggs and egg yolks together and pour them into the well, then incorporate them into the flour using a fork. You may need to add an extra yolk if the dough is too dry. Knead the dough until it is shiny and firm to the touch, for at least 10 minutes. Form the dough into a ball, then wrap it in plastic wrap and refrigerate it for 30 minutes.

Divide the dough into four. Using a pasta machine, feed a piece of dough through the widest aperture 8–10 times until shiny and silky, folding the ends in over each other between each rolling. Pass the dough through each of the remaining settings 3–4 times until you reach the second-to-last setting. Run the pasta sheets through your chosen cutters. Cover the pasta with plastic wrap if you plan to cook it immediately, otherwise see the note below about drying pasta.

Bring the water to a boil in a tall pot, then add salt. Slide the pasta gently into the pot as the water returns to a boil, then partially cover with a lid to bring it to a rapid boil. Fresh pasta only needs to cook for 3 minutes or so. Stir the pasta gently to keep it well separated (a tablespoon of olive oil in the water can help too). Drain the cooked pasta—this is easiest if you have a colander for this purpose that fits inside your pot—and reserve a little of the cooking water in case you want to moisten the completed dish. Do not run the cooked pasta under water as you will lose the precious starch that helps the sauce or oil adhere.

MAKES 1 pound 2 ounces

DRYING PASTA

If you are not cooking the pasta immediately, it is important that you dry it for about 3 hours. To do this, hang the strips of pasta over the back of a chair or a broom handle suspended between two chairs, making sure that the strips are not touching. Slip the dried pasta onto a tray and cook as above (it will take a little longer than just-made pasta).

HERBED PASTA

The pasta dough given on page 211 can also incorporate freshly chopped herbs to give it another dimension. If you want to give the pasta a speckled effect, then a small quantity of a "dry" herb such as rosemary can be cut very finely and worked into the flour. If you want to color the pasta, then "wet" herbs such as parsley, sorrel, or basil (or vegetables such as spinach or spring onions) are used. You need to use more of these herbs than if making "speckled" pasta (perhaps a handful, which is then chopped), and you won't need to use as many eggs. Try omitting one of the eggs to start with—you may find you need to add a little extra yolk if the dough is too dry.

Sauces

MAYONNAISE

Italians make mayonnaise with olive oil and eggs and sometimes lemon juice. They do not put mustard in it, although they may very well add cooked chopped spinach, herbs, or tuna. One of the best-known Italian ways with mayonnaise is in making the sauce for *Vitello Tonnato* (see page 126).

3 egg yolks
pinch of salt
lemon juice or white-wine vinegar
1¼ cups olive oil
white pepper or Tabasco

Choose a comfortable basin and rest it on a damp cloth, so it cannot slip around. Work the egg yolks with the salt and 1 tablespoon lemon juice for a minute until smooth. Gradually beat in the olive oil using a wooden spoon—add the first few tablespoons one at a time and beat very well after each. After a third of the oil has been added, the rest can be added in a thin, steady stream, beating all the while. (This is easiest to do if you have a helper to pour while you beat.) Taste for acidity and adjust with drops of lemon juice, salt, and pepper. If you have prepared the mayonnaise ahead, refrigerate it with plastic wrap pressed onto the surface to prevent a skin forming. Allow the mayonnaise to return to room temperature before serving, and stir to ensure it is smooth.

MAKES 1½ CUPS

FOOD PROCESSOR

Mayonnaise can also be made well in a food processor or blender. However, it absorbs a lot more air this way and will never have the same "glop" or yellow sheen to it as when made by hand. Simply follow the procedure above, blending the eggs and salt first, then adding the oil gradually with the motor running.

PESTO

Pesto originated in Genoa on the Ligurian coast to the northwest of Tuscany, but the principle of grinding or chopping nuts, garlic, herbs, and cheese and adding oil is one found throughout Italy. *Pesto* makes a great alternative to *Salsa Agresto* (see page 23) when serving vegetables and meat from the grill.

1 cup pine nuts

¾ cup extra-virgin olive oil

2 cloves garlic

1 packed cup basil leaves

salt

freshly ground black pepper

¼ cup freshly grated Parmigiano-Reggiano

¼ cup freshly grated pecorino

Dry-roast the pine nuts in a frying pan until golden, tossing frequently to prevent burning. Put ¼ cup of the olive oil and all the ingredients except the cheese into a food processor and blend to a paste, then check the seasoning and stir in the remaining oil and the cheese.

MAKES 1½ CUPS

Stock

BRODO

Italian broth or *brodo* is thinner in consistency and less concentrated than stock made in the French manner. It often consists of a mixture of raw meat and poultry bones and trimmings, which gives it its delicacy.

It is not usual in Italian cookery to reduce broth to a coating sauce, or to beat a lot of butter or cream into it.

2¼ pounds chopped veal or beef bones (or a mixture)
    plus any leftover trimmings (fat, gristle, etc.)

1 boiling fowl (including giblets)

1 carrot, peeled and chopped

1 onion, peeled and chopped

1 stick celery

1 leek, washed and sliced

3 stalks parsley

1 bay leaf

1 sprig thyme

1 large tomato, halved and seeded

Put all the ingredients into a large stockpot and cover generously with cold water. Bring slowly to a boil and skim off all foam and scum. Reduce the pan to a simmer and cook for 4 hours at a bare shiver, then strain and allow to cool, uncovered. Refrigerate the cooled *brodo* and remove any congealed fat from the surface. Use the *brodo* within a few days or reboil it. Season only when the dish it is being used in is nearing completion.

MAKES 3 QUARTS

FLAVORING

A more specific flavor can be achieved by adding squab, quail, or rabbit trimmings to the completed *brodo*. Add more vegetables and additional water to cover. Bring to simmering point, then skim and allow to simmer at a bare shiver for 2 hours.

CHICKEN BRODO

The chicken *brodo* we made during the cooking school sessions was delicious. It must have had something to do with the boiling fowls we used—they were much more flavorsome than the hens to which we are accustomed.

1 boiling fowl, 4½ pounds

2 carrots, chopped

2 sticks celery, trimmed and chopped

3 large brown onions, chopped

3 sprigs parsley

2 sprigs thyme

2 cloves garlic

4 black peppercorns

salt

Put all the ingredients except the salt into a large stockpot and cover generously with water. Bring slowly to a boil, then skim off any foam and scum. Reduce the pan to a simmer and cook for 2 hours at a bare shiver, then strain and season with salt. Remove the chicken from the bones and reserve for another use. Refrigerate the cooled *brodo* and remove any congealed fat from the surface once cold. Use the *brodo* within a day or so or reboil it.

MAKES 2–3 QUARTS

FISH BRODO

This is the base broth we used when making our fish stew (see page 116). We also used it to alter the character of the *Risotto Radicchio* on page 93.

> 1½ tablespoons unsalted butter
>
> 1 large onion, finely chopped
>
> 1 leek, washed and finely chopped
>
> 1 carrot, finely chopped
>
> ½ stick celery, finely chopped
>
> 2¼ pounds snapper heads, cleaned and roughly
> chopped
>
> ½ cup dry white wine
>
> 4–6 cups cold water
>
> 10 stalks Italian (flat-leaved) parsley, chopped
>
> 1 sprig thyme
>
> ½ bay leaf
>
> ½ teaspoon powdered saffron (optional)

Melt the butter in a large stockpot, then add all the vegetables and sweat for 2 minutes without browning. Add the snapper heads and sweat for another minute. Pour in the white wine and boil vigorously for a few minutes, then add the cold water, herbs, and saffron, if using. Simmer for 20 minutes. Strain through a sieve or muslin, pressing down gently on the bones and vegetables. Allow to cool and then refrigerate. Use within the day.

MAKES 1 QUART

Tomatoes

CONFIT OF TOMATOES

These slow-roasted tomatoes are wonderful with goat cheese, in a salad with smoked or marinated salmon, in pasta with anchovies, or in an octopus salad with arugula.

> *ripe plum tomatoes*
>
> *extra-virgin olive oil*
>
> *basil leaves*
>
> *sprigs of thyme*
>
> *garlic cloves, peeled*
>
> *best-quality sea salt*
>
> *freshly ground black pepper*

Preheat the oven to 200°F. Cut the tomatoes in half lengthwise. Take a baking dish that will accommodate the tomatoes in a single layer and oil it generously with extra-virgin olive oil. Arrange a layer of overlapping basil leaves, thyme sprigs, and peeled garlic cloves over the base of the dish, then add the tomatoes, cut-side down. Sprinkle generously with sea salt and pepper and drizzle with more olive oil. Bake, covered, for 5 hours, then allow to cool completely. These tomatoes are delicious and will last well for 3–4 days.

'STRATTU

MAGGIE ❧ I first learned of *'strattu* from Mary Taylor Simetti's book *Pomp and Sustenance*. For this, tomatoes are puréed and salted and then dried in the sun, where they are stirred frequently until all moisture has evaporated. *'Strattu* is traditionally prepared without any cooking, but it can also be cooked initially to speed up the process. The raw version has a fresher, more acidic taste, and is a vibrant red rather than rust-colored but it takes about a week to complete. Cooking the mixture first halves the preparation time.

The tomatoes used must be super-ripe and have no "off" characteristics or blemishes as these will spoil the end product. Plum tomatoes are best to use as they contain less moisture than others, and therefore make a dense purée that won't run when it is put out to dry. If altering the quantities given here, note that 26 pounds tomatoes produces 2 pounds 'strattu and that salt is added at 1.5 percent of the weight of the tomatoes.

> 26 pounds ripe plum tomatoes
> ¾ cup salt
> sprigs of basil (optional)
> olive oil

Wash the tomatoes and remove their stems, then cut the flesh into small pieces. Pass the tomato through a food mill to remove the skin and seeds, then salt the purée. You can also add sprigs of basil at this stage, if desired.

Spread the fresh purée over a clean wooden table in full sun using a plastic pastry scraper. (If you have not used plum tomatoes, you may need to start the drying on trays to prevent the purée running off the table.) Stir and gather the purée with the scraper every time you pass by to help it dry out. The number of times the purée is attended to will determine how long it takes to dry. You will need to bring the table inside at night to prevent the purée becoming damp.

When the 'strattu is thick like clay, remove the basil (if added) and pack the mixture into sterilized glass jars, pressing down to remove any air bubbles, then pour in olive oil to seal. The 'strattu will last for months until opened.

MAKES 2 POUNDS

TO COOK FIRST

To reduce the drying period, cook the tomato purée first. Choose an enameled or stainless steel pot and boil a small amount of the purée (the tomato sticks easily and burns) until it has reduced, then add more purée and so on. Add the salt to the reduced purée and transfer the mixture to the table top and proceed as above.

SUN-DRIED TOMATOES

The tomatoes you choose to dry or semidry must have been left to ripen fully on the vine. This is more important even than the variety of the tomato. If the tomatoes are large, cut them into 1-inch-thick slices, and cut plum tomatoes in half lengthwise. Cherry tomatoes can be halved or picked as a bunch and left to dry whole (although this can take quite a while).

Sprinkle the tomatoes with a little sea salt (being careful not to oversalt them) and dry them on racks in the sun for 2–3 days, less for semidried tomatoes, bringing them in at night to avoid the dew. Protect the tomatoes from flies with muslin or fine wire netting. And don't let the tomatoes become too dark and overdry.

Instead of drying the tomatoes in the sun, a dehydrator or electric dryer can be used—the process will take 3–4 hours, depending on the thickness of the tomatoes. Another option is to dry them out overnight in an oven with the pilot light left on.

Sun-dried tomatoes have an extended shelf-life, while semidried tomatoes deteriorate more quickly and need to be refrigerated. Both should be stored in olive oil.

GARLIC

The sliced or halved tomatoes can also be layered with garlic, salt, and pepper when drying in the sun, before being added to an *antipasto* platter as semidried tomatoes or stored in oil.

STUFFED SUN-DRIED TOMATOES

A great way of using sun-dried tomatoes is given in Patience Gray's *Honey from a Weed*. There she "stuffs" sun-dried tomatoes with anchovies, capers, or fennel seeds and stores them in olive oil with fresh bay leaves as an *antipasto* treat. Plum tomatoes are best for this—the tomato is sliced through to the stem, which is left intact, and the stuffing is sandwiched between the two halves.

Glossary

The following list of words and phrases includes Italian culinary terms and ingredients that may not be known to all readers. The Italian words are highlighted in *italic* type, while **bold** type indicates that an entry for that word appears in this list. This is by no means a comprehensive guide to Italian culinary terms and ingredients, but rather a record of those used in this book.

acidulated water
Water to which lemon juice, slices of lemon, or vinegar has been added. Immersing certain peeled vegetables and fruit (for example, **artichokes**) in acidulated water prevents discoloration.

al dente
Literally "to the tooth." Used to describe the "doneness" of **pasta** or *risotto*, which should be left with a little resistance to the bite after cooking.

amaretti
Light, crisp cookies like macaroons flavored with bitter almonds or apricot kernels.

Amaro
A dark Italian digestif native to the Abruzzo region and made from herbs.

anchovies
Look for Spanish and Italian brands of anchovies that are packed in olive oil; they are widely available. Less ubiquitous, but a delicious treat when found in specialty food stores, are anchovies packed in salt. Salted anchovies need to be rinsed thoroughly before use in cooking, however.

antipasto
Literally "before the meal." A collection of meats (*salami*), pickled or grilled vegetables (olives, eggplant, **artichokes**), *frittata*, and so on served as a starter to whet the appetite.

arborio
A medium- to short-grained rice used to make *risotto*. Its high starch levels produce the creaminess essential to this dish. There are other specialty rice varieties also intended for *risotto*, among them *carnaroli* and *vialone*.

artichoke
The flower head of the globe artichoke is used in a variety of ways in Italian cooking: stewed, poached, stuffed, or fried, for example. Tiny young artichokes are also tender enough to be used raw in salads. Artichokes need to be immersed in **acidulated water** to prevent discoloration once cut.

arugula/rugula/rucola
A peppery salad leaf also known as rocket.

beans
Tuscans are called *mangiafagioli* (bean eaters) for good reason: they use both fresh and dried beans in soups and stews and in braises and purées served as side dishes or toppings for *crostini* or *bruschetta*. In Italy we used the beautiful deep-pink and cream *borlotti* (cranberry) beans and the smaller cream *cannellini*, available both dried and fresh, in season. The fresh beans are well worth looking for, or growing, although the dried can be substituted with ease. Dried beans need to be soaked overnight and then cooked for about 1½ hours, while fresh beans need no soaking and are cooked for 45 minutes.

biscotti
Cookies, or, more precisely, the "twice-cooked" cookies of Tuscany.

bocconcini
Tiny, round fresh cheeses that are uncured and unripened. They are usually sold in brine and are most often sliced and served as part of an *antipasto* platter or in a salad.

borlotti see beans

broccoli rabe
Also known as *rapini*, *broccoletti di rape*, rape, and Italian turnip. A dark-green, leafy vegetable related to the turnip and flowering broccoli, it has a slightly nutty flavor and can be chopped and sautéed and served as a side dish or added to a *risotto*, and so on. From one of the *Brassica rapa* groups, it is not to be confused with *B. napus* and *B. campestris*, formerly known as rape and grown for the seed used to make canola oil.

brodo
Broth or stock, although much lighter than the long-cooked and reduced French version. Used to make *minestre* (soup) and *risotto*.

Brunello di Montalcino
A big, dry red wine made from a clone of the Sangiovese grape that has adapted particularly well to the area around Montalcino. According to **DOCG** regulations, Brunello di Montalcino must be aged in the barrel for a minimum of three years and is sold after a total of four years' aging.

bruschetta
Slices of dense bread that are grilled either over coals or on a cast-iron grill and then topped with any variety of ingredients. The char marks are part of the charm, as is the charcoal flavor. See also *crostini*.

cannellini see beans

capers
The preserved flower buds of the caper bush, native to the Mediterranean region. Look for the tiny capers from the Aeolian islands off Sicily that come packed in brine or salt, both of which are preferable to the inferior vinegar of many cheaper alternatives. If salted, the capers need to be rinsed thoroughly but gently before use—dunking a sieve into a bowl of clean water several times rinses the salt without disturbing the bud.

caprese
Literally "from Capri" and the name given to a salad made from green-shouldered tomatoes, *mozzarella*, and basil and dressed with best-quality extra-virgin **olive oil**.

cardoons
A member of the thistle family and related to the globe **artichoke**, which it also resembles in flavor, although the young, solid stalks are eaten rather than the flower. Stripped of any tough strings and trimmed of spiky edges before being peeled, the stalks are parboiled before being braised or baked. Cardoons can be grown, but are rarely seen for sale outside of Italy.

carpaccio
Traditionally paper-thin slices of raw beef fillet served with mayonnaise, but now extended to include fish.

cavolo nero
The long-leafed, green-blue cabbage of Tuscany, and a traditional ingredient in *minestrone*. It has a pleasantly bitter flavor and withstands long cooking, during which time it deepens in color until almost black. Not widely available, so try Savoy cabbage in its place, although quite a different flavor will result.

Chianti
The region in Tuscany between Siena in the south and Florence in the north that is famous for the red wine of the same name. Sold in flasks, the fresh, young Chianti is a blend of Sangiovese (the main grape grown in the region), Trebbiano, Malvasia, and perhaps Canaiolo. In some cases, the unfermented must of dried grapes (*il governo*) is added to the fermented juice to introduce a touch of fizz. The best Chianti is made without *il governo* and is aged for three years in oak or tanks and then bottles and is released as Riserva. See also **Chianti Classico**.

Chianti Classico
A dry red wine from a specific region of the **Chianti** made traditionally from Sangiovese grapes (but also now allowed to include up to 10 percent of nontraditional varieties such as Cabernet Sauvignon, Merlot or Shiraz) and no more than 5 percent white grape varieties.

Classified **DOCG**, Chianti Classico is thought to be one of the best wines in Italy. It is aged in oak for a year and bottle-aged for an additional 12 months. Chianti Classico wines carry the *gallo nero* or black cockerel seal around the neck of the bottle. See also **Chianti**.

cinghiale
Wild boar found in Italy's forests. A sweet, veal-like meat used in pasta sauces and stews, it can be marinated and roasted, made into sausages, or cured to become **prosciutto**.

corn salad
Also known as *lamb's lettuce* (U.K.), *mache* (France), or *valeriana* (Italy). A velvety-leafed salad green with a rather bitter taste that often grows wild. The clusters of leaves should be picked when young.

crespelle
Very thin pancakes or *crêpes* that are stuffed with either a savory or sweet filling.

crostini
Thin slices of bread with a thinnish crust (from a baguette, for example) that are either toasted under a grill, crisped in the oven or fried in **olive oil** or butter. *Crostoni* are simply larger versions of *crostini*.

crostoni see crostini

cuttlefish
Related to squid, cuttlefish are readily available in Italian markets, but less so outside of Italy. The sweet flesh is equally delicious braised or grilled. As with squid, braising takes considerably longer than grilling for the flesh to become tender.

DOC/DOCG
The Denominazione di Origine Controllata/ Garantita—the regulatory system for Italy's regional produce (including wine, **prosciutto**, balsamic vinegar, cheese, and, more recently, **olive oil**). When referring to wines, DOC has dictated viticultural and wine-making practices since it was brought in in the 1960s (for example, defining regions, grape varieties, tonnages, alcohol levels, aging, and so on). "Garantita" signifies the very best of Italian wines, as rated by the DOC, and includes Albana di Romagna, Barbaresco, Barolo, **Brunello di Montalcino**, **Chianti Classico**, and Vino Nobile di Montepulciano. Any wine not made to DOC regulations is labeled *vino da tavola*, table or everyday wine. This may or may not reflect the true nature of the wine or the aspirations of the winemaker. It must be said that there are some very fine wines made outside DOC guidelines, in particular the super-Tuscans. See also *Parmigiano-Reggiano*.

fennel
Available as seeds or fresh as a bulb, which can be eaten raw or braised, fried, and so on. Both the bulb and the seeds have an aniseed flavor and are said to be good for the digestion, which is why the bulb is often eaten raw at the end of a meal instead of fruit in Italy. The seeds are also added to **salami**, particularly the Tuscan specialty, *finocchiona*.

gamberetti
Tiny Mediterranean shrimp that require little else than a minute's boiling before being seasoned and served as part of an **antipasto** platter. They can be eaten shells and all.

gelato
Italian ice-cream, made either with sugar syrup or cream and/or egg yolks as its base. The plural is *gelati*.

gnocchi
Small dumplings made from a dough of potato or flour (and sometimes with the addition of a puréed vegetable such as squash or spinach) that are poached quickly and partnered with a sauce. Also refers to a shape of pasta shell.

gorgonzola
A strongly flavored creamy blue cheese made from cow's milk. Stainless steel or copper wires are inserted into the maturing cheese to ensure the mold spreads evenly.

grappa
The equivalent of France's *marc*. A spirit distilled from the grape skins and pips left in the wine press. A shot of *grappa* in coffee produces *caffè corretto*.

gremolata
A mixture of finely diced lemon zest, garlic, and parsley that is often added to braised dishes, especially *osso buco*, just before serving.

grissini
Pencil-thin breadsticks that form part of an **antipasto** platter or that accompany **pinzimonio**.

lasagne
Sheets of cooked pasta layered most usually with a meat or vegetable filling, cheese, and béchamel sauce and baked until bubbling and golden. *Lasagna*, the singular, refers to a sheet of the pasta.

limoncello
A spirit from Capri that has been distilled from grain and infused with lemon zest.

mascarpone
A fresh and very rich soft cream cheese made from cow's milk. Italian *mascarpone* is much creamier and thicker than American versions.

melanzane
Eggplant.

mezzaluna
Literally "half moon." The curved and double-handled knife used to chop garlic and so on.

minestrone
A thick vegetable soup that usually includes **beans** and perhaps **pasta**. Tuscan *minestrone* usually includes *cavolo nero*, a green-blue cabbage. *Minestra* means "soup." *Minestrina* is a broth.

mortadella
A large, cooked sausage from Bologna. It combines pork and beef in a delicate, smooth mix and has one of the highest fat contents of all cooked sausages. Some versions include peppercorns, others pistachios. It is usually sliced and served as is but it can also be diced and added to sauces, pasta stuffings, or sautés.

mostarda di Cremona
A condiment originally from Cremona in Lombardy and traditionally served with *bollito misto*, a selection of boiled meats and vegetables. Fruit such as apricots, peaches, pears, cherries, and figs are preserved in a syrup flavored with mustard.

mozzarella
A fresh cheese with excellent melting qualities traditionally made from buffalo milk in southern Italy, and now increasingly available from a variety of American cheese producers.

myrtle
The leaves of the myrtle tree are used to impart a mildly resinous flavor to game and roasted meat in Mediterranean countries. The peppery dried blue-black berries can also be crushed and used as one does juniper berries.

olive oil
Olive oils have a wide variety of flavors ranging from light and buttery to very fruity. The color also varies from a deep green-gold to light gold. The deeper the color, the fuller the flavor. The flavor and color depend on the quality and variety of the olive, the climate and soil in which the tree grew, the care with which the tree was cultivated, how the oil was extracted, and how well it was stored. Tuscan olive oils are famous for their fruity flavor and a characteristic touch of pepper, signs of a cooler growing season.

Extra-virgin olive oil, from the first pressing, must have less than 1 percent acidity expressed as free oleic acid (sometimes described as "free fatty acid"). It must also not have any flavor defects. Virgin olive oil may not exceed 1.5 percent acidity. The olive oil that does not fit either criterion is refined and then has virgin olive oil blended into it to restore flavor and color—this is sold as refined or "pure" olive oil.

Best-quality extra-virgin olive oil is a revelation to anyone used to chemically treated refined oils. Such oil is highly valued in Italy, and contributes as much to a dish such as *panzanella* (see page 181) as do the full-flavored tomatoes. Excellent local and imported extra-virgin olive oils are now widely available in the United States. Use this oil for dressing dishes when flavor is important, and use a virgin olive oil for cooking.

osteria see trattoria

pancetta
The belly of the pig cured and often rolled but not smoked. A version is also cured with cayenne pepper. Serve thinly sliced or cut into thick rounds for dicing and adding to sauces.

panettone
A yeast cake from Milan flavored with candied peel and dried fruit that can be served plain or toasted.

panforte
A dense, sweet, spicy cake native to Siena that is made with candied peel, nuts, honey, sometimes cocoa, and a tiny amount of flour.

panna cotta
Literally "cooked cream." A delicately flavored dessert made with milk and cream and set in individual molds.

panzanella
A rustic Tuscan salad usually made with day-old bread, tomato, onion, celery, cucumber, garlic, basil, and a vinaigrette of red-wine vinegar and extra-virgin **olive oil**. The quality of the ingredients determines the outcome of the dish.

panzarotti
Little fried olive-oil pastry pasties filled with a mixture, such as cheese and ham or *salami*.

pappa al pomodoro
A rustic Tuscan soup that uses day-old bread, tomato and **brodo** as its main ingredients.

Parmigiano-Reggiano
Italy's finest parmesan cheese produced under the strictly delineated **DOC** in northern Italy. A *grana* (grainy cheese), this spicy, sweet, and nutty cheese is made from April to November each year from the milk of cows that have been grazing on fresh grass. Whole milk from the morning's milking is mixed with partially skimmed milk from the previous evening's milking. No chemicals or coloring agents can be used, and rennet and salt are the only additives permitted. The newly formed cheeses are soaked in brine, hence the allowance of salt. Each *Parmigiano-Reggiano* wheel must weigh no less than 72 pounds and no more than 100 pounds, and each must be aged for at least fourteen months. A three-year-old *Parmigiano-Reggiano* is known as *stravecchio* ("very old") and a four-year-old cheese is referred to as *stravecchione* ("even older!").

Independent inspectors regularly check the cheeses for any faults; the approved wheels are branded with a hot iron (the oval seal of the consortium certifies the month and year of production), while dotted matrix insignia declaring the cheese to be *Parmigiano-Reggiano* appear over the entire rind. The wheel may also carry an export stamp of quality.

There are many other *grana* cheeses made in northern Italy, but they cannot legally be referred to as *Parmigiano-Reggiano*. Two other well-known cheeses are *grana padano* (milder and cheaper than *Parmigiano-Reggiano*, it is aged for six months and is especially good for grating) and *pecorino* (the classic grating sheep's milk cheese of southern Italy).

passata
A fresh tomato sauce made from tomatoes that have been put through a food mill.

pasta
Available fresh or dried and in more than three hundred shapes. Some shapes are only sold dried (tubular varieties), while other types are sold both dried and fresh (*linguine, tagliatelle, fettuccine, spaghetti, lasagne*). Fresh pasta can be kneaded and cut by hand or a hand-operated pasta machine can be used (see page 211). Commercially produced pasta is mixed and kneaded by machine and the paste is shaped or extruded by huge metal rollers. If the rollers are stainless steel or Teflon, the pasta will have a smooth finish. If the rollers are bronze, the pasta will be more textured and will look duller. Bronze-extruded pasta is considered superior, as the rougher texture enables more sauce to cling to the pasta.

Durum wheat, which grinds down to **semolina**, is the grain preferred in the south of Italy and is particularly suited to dried pasta, which requires longer cooking. In the north of Italy it is traditional to make pasta such as *fettuccine, tagliatelle,* and *linguine* with softer wheat flours mixed with egg for a faster-cooking pasta. American dried pasta is of acceptable quality due to the durum wheat grown here, but it is also well worth the effort to make your own pasta.

pecorino
A sheep's milk cheese that can either be sold fresh or aged, of which *pecorino romano*, for grating, is perhaps the best known.

pesto
A sauce of garlic, pine nuts, and basil pounded together and bound with **olive oil** and **Parmigiano-Reggiano**. *Pesto* originated in Genoa and is traditionally tossed through hot spaghetti but is also good as a substitute for **salsa agresto** (see page 23).

piadina
A flatbread baked on a terra-cotta tile or **testa** and similar to the Indian *roti*.

pinzimonio
The Italian version of the French crudités. Raw, young vegetables are dipped into good **olive oil**, sea salt, and pepper as an appetizer.

polenta
Also known as cornmeal. Cooked with varying amounts of water and/or stock (and sometimes milk) and often flavored with butter and *Parmigiano-Reggiano*. Served either as a soft side dish or allowed to set and then cut into wedges and grilled or baked.

polpettine
Little meatballs often flavored with *Parmigiano-Reggiano* and herbs.

porcini
Literally "little pig." Known in France as *cèpes*, these meaty mushrooms are available in Europe fresh or dried and have smooth, tan-colored caps and pale, thick stems. Dried *porcini* are widely available in the United States and increasing numbers of gourmet grocers stock the mushrooms fresh.

Use field mushrooms in the place of fresh *porcini*, but expect a different result, or else try the mushrooms sold as slippery jacks, Blue Mountain cèpes, and other regional names. These are *Suillus luteus* and *S. granulatus*, which belong to the *Boletus* genus, as does the *porcini*, and have a flavor between a field mushroom and poached bone marrow.

Dried *porcini* need to be reconstituted in water for about 20 minutes before use. The soaking water can be strained and used to flavor stocks, soup, or *risotto*.

prosciutto crudo
Literally "raw ham," as opposed to *prosciutto cotto* (cooked ham). An important difference to learn when shopping in Italy as a request for *prosciutto* alone will confuse.

provolone
A cow's milk cheese traditionally made in southern Italy. Most is aged for a few months, while some is aged to six months or more, the older cheeses being used for grating. A nutty cheese with a firm texture suited to cooking.

radicchio
A chicory, *radicchio* comes in shades of red, green, cream, and variegated. There are hearted (for example, *radicchio di Chioggia*) and loose-leafed varieties (*radicchio di Treviso*). *Radicchio* can be bitter and can take a strong dressing or be grilled and fried. It can also be added to cooked dishes such as *risotto*. *Radicchio di Treviso* is a particular favorite but is not widely available, although the seeds are available for home gardeners.

ravioli
A stuffed **pasta** in the form of little pillows that usually contain a meat, vegetable, or cheese filling. *Ravioli* are poached and then sometimes baked.

ribollita
Literally "reboiled." *Minestrone* reheated with bread added to it becomes *ribollita*.

ricotta
Literally "recooked." A fresh, grainy cheese most often made by heating the whey drained off when making cheeses such as *mozzarella* and *provolone*, and then skimming off the solids which rise to the top.

risotto
A dish in which rice is cooked gently with the gradual addition of hot stock and frequent stirring. *Arborio*, *carnaroli*, or *vialone* rice are used when making *risotto*, which needs a starchy rice with a firm texture to endure the slow cooking. Vegetables, seafood, and so on can be added to *risotto* to alter its character.

ristorante see *trattoria*

rotolo
Literally "roll." A large **pasta** sheet is covered with a filling and then rolled up to form a log before being poached and sliced.

salame/salami
The supreme dried sausage. True *salami* is made from uncooked meat and may or may not be smoked. Most is made from fresh pork and has a coarsely ground texture with garlic as the main spice. The types and amount of meat used; the proportion of lean to fat; how finely, coarsely, or uniformly the fat appears among the lean; the choice of seasoning; and the degree of salting and drying dictate the nature of the *salami*. *Salame calabrese* is a hot, spicy sausage that includes chilies, red wine, and red peppers and is air-dried, whereas the style of *salame alla casalinga* ("homemade") depends on where "home" is for the person who made it. *Soppressa di salame* includes pork and beef and is highly regarded. A coarsely textured, air-dried sausage, it is tied with string to create its traditional bulging shape. *Finocchiona*, a Tuscan specialty, is a soft salame flavored with fennel seeds.

salsa agresto
A paste made from walnuts, almonds, parsley, and basil in the style of **pesto**—but with the addition of **verjuice**—and served with grilled vegetables and meats.

semifreddo
Literally "semicold." A creamy dessert that is chilled until partially frozen.

semolina
The milled endosperm of wheat. Fine semolina is used to make a type of *gnocchi*, while medium-ground semolina is used to make desserts and cakes. Durum wheat semolina is used to make commercial **pasta**.

sformato
Literally "shapeless" or "disfigured." In a culinary sense, it refers to a molded pudding or similar.

sponge ladyfinger cookies
Known in Italian as *biscotti savoiardi*. A light cookie used for desserts, often dipped into or sprinkled with liqueur and layered with cream or *mascarpone*. *Tirami su* is the best-known example.

stracciatella alla romana
Chicken **brodo** that has had an egg whisked through it with *Parmigiano-Reggiano* and served as a soup. *Stracciatella* literally means "rags." See also *zuppa pavese*.

'strattu
A concentrated tomato paste obtained by drying puréed tomato in the sun over a number of days.

Strega
A rich, aged Italian digestif made from herbs and spices.

super-Tuscans see DOC/DOCG

testa
The terra-cotta tile on which a *piadina* is cooked.

trattoria
Basically a cheaper version of a *ristorante*, and with more choices than a *pizzeria* or perhaps an *osteria* (a wine bar/*trattoria*).

truffle
White truffles (*tartufi bianchi*) are found during the Italian autumn and winter in the forests of Tuscany, Piedmont, and Emilia-Romagna. A type of fungi, they can be as large as a tennis ball and are not white but brownish, but certainly much lighter in color than the less fragrant black truffle. White truffles have an unforgettable, persistent earthy aroma and flavor and their rarity makes them extremely expensive. They are used raw and extremely simply, shaved over fresh **pasta** or *risotto* or into scrambled eggs, for example. A truffle slicer is an essential device for anyone who has regular access to truffles. A fresh truffle can be stored in a container of rice or *polenta* for a day or two or with eggs for longer (up to a week, if you can wait that long!) to impart its unique flavor. Truffles are flown into the United States in season (winter, roughly December to March), although for

vast sums of money, and are preferred over the imported canned varieties. Enthusiasts have begun cultivation of Périgord black truffles on the East Coast of the United States, but they are not yet widely available.

verjuice/agresto
The juice of unripe grapes used as an acidulant (for example, in a vinaigrette), in sauce-making or when cooking poultry or fish. Verjuice has the tartness of lemon and the acidity of vinegar without the harshness of either and lends a subtle flavor of grapes. Available from French gourmet stores under the name *verjus*. Lemon juice or "softer" vinegars (such as rice wine) may be substituted in a pinch. See also *salsa agresto*.

vin santo
Literally "holy wine" and a specialty of Tuscany. A sweet amber-colored dessert wine produced from a variety of grapes (Trebbiano and Malvasia predominantly) that are picked ripe and then left to dry for four months on bamboo racks. The shriveled fruit is crushed to produce a small amount of juice that is then transferred to oak barrels with its lees (sediment), where it rests for four years before being blended and bottled. The barrels are never cleaned of old lees. New *vin santo* juice is added and the process starts again.

vino
Wine—*vino rosso* (red), *vino bianco* (white), and *vino rosa* (rosé). See also *vin santo*.

vitello tonnato
Literally "veal and tuna." A cold veal salad in which finely sliced poached veal is coated in a sauce made from mayonnaise, tuna, **anchovies,** and **capers.** Traditionally the dish is decorated with anchovies, olives, capers, and thinly sliced lemon.

zuccotto
Thought to have been inspired by the dome of Florence's cathedral, this dessert comprises layers of whipped cream or *mascarpone* flavored with chocolate, nuts, and candied peel in a basin lined with liqueur-moistened cake. The dessert is unmolded onto a platter for serving.

zuppa pavese
Based on chicken **brodo**, this soup can include *Parmigiano-Reggiano* and a whole egg poached in the broth (if an egg is stirred into the broth, the soup becomes *stracciatella alla romana*). A more sophisticated version includes wraps of lettuce stuffed with chicken.

Index

Laurel Glen Publishing
An imprint of the Advantage Publishers Group
5880 Oberlin Drive, San Diego, CA 92121-4794
www.advantagebooksonline.com

ISBN 1-57145-686-4

Library of Congress Cataloging-in-Publication Data

Alexander, Stephanie, 1940-
Stephanie Alexander & Maggie Beer's Tuscan Cookbook/photography by Simon Griffiths.
p. cm.
Includes bibliographical references.
ISBN 1-57145-686-4
1. Cookery, Italian--Tuscan style. I. Title: Tuscan cookbook. II. Beer, Magie. III. Title.

TX723.2.T86 T45 2001
641.5945'5--dc21
20011035311

Design by Beth McKinlay
Photography by Simon Griffiths
Typeset in Giovanni 10/16pt
Americanization by TransAtlantic Chef
Printed and bound by South China Printing Co Ltd, Hong Kong

1 2 3 4 5   01 02 03 04 05